MEL BAY'S

OLD-TIME COWBOY SONGBOOK

BY WILL McCAIN CLAUSON

Cover Credit:
Charles M. Russel/Superstock, Inc.

G000298270

DEDICATION

TO THE FAMILY,

YOURS AN' MINE.

To my loving Parents,

John an' Marie.

My Sons,

Juanito an' Patrick

an' their Mother,

Christina.

ACKNOWLEDGMENTS

I would like to express my deepest gratitude to the many people who have made this book possible. To Alice Krause and Howard Culver for their concern and helpfulness as authorities on the Old West, having been a part it. To Aaron Keegan for sharing with me the cowboy vernacular and insisting that "most cowboys sang some." To Waldo "Swede" Larson, Lloyd "Bucksin" Robinson, and Travis "Nick" Merritt for their cowboy expertise.

To Rick Steiner for helping me find some "lost chords" in my arrangements. To Tommy Cropper, for transcribing the songs on to the computer. To Carol Steinway for helping me research cowboy dances. To Juanita Bayne and Sherry Mundy for their able assistance in getting my scattered thoughts and bits and pieces into print. To the innumerable others who have been so helpful in contributing their versions of traditional songs.

To my mentor, Carl Sandburg, the great American poet and folk scholar, who sparked my interest in collecting and singing songs in the folk idiom.

I am deeply indebted to Mr. Anonymous and Mr. Unknown, who have been writing for me, so to speak, for the past one-hundred years, more or less. This book could never have been written without their help.

I also give thanks to Katie Lee, Burl Ives, Robert and Julie Mitchum, Pete Seeger, the Clancy Brothers, Josh White, and to Judge Liam DeVally for helping me trace some of the cowboy melodies back to the "ould sod." To Trio Calaveras, who gave me the songs of the Mexican Charros, and to Mario De La Piedra, who further helped and inspired me in my research. Finally, to all my other "singing compadres," of the past and present, who have generously shared their songs with me.

Also, I would like to recognize my publisher, Bill Bay, who has already done so much for the preservation of historic songs. It is an honor for me to be a small part of adding to his vast collection.

ABOUT THE AUTHOR

Will McCain Clauson's career has spanned the Globe. He has performed on every Continent, with the exception of Antarctica...from the Grand Ol' Opry in Nashville, to appearing as one of the few unaccompanied solo artists to be featured at Carnegie Hall in New York, and the Royal Festival Hall in London.

Will has over sixty albums on major labels to his credit, two of which went gold. He is an Award winning ASCAP author, and composer of long standing.

Stories, music, and history flourish in his "Old Time Cowboy Song Book."

- Juanita Bayne

"William Clauson is a Viking of Song, to me irresistible, one of the most colorful and versatile singers and accomplished guitarists I have ever heard."

- Carl Sandburg

"Will McCain Clauson has given us "wanna-be" cowboys a new taste of the Ol' West. He has successfully joined the myth and reality of the American Cowboy."

- Jim Bottoms, M.A.
Regent University
Director, The Theatre Troupe

I took pleasure, both as a professional, and as the daughter of pioneers, in reliving the Golden Days of the West through your collection of music, history, and legends of the people who lived them.

...an important chronicle of bygone days, filling a long-vacant niche in our country's history...truly a CELEBRATION of the words and music of the Old West.

- Valle Novak
Arts Editor
Bonner County Daily Bee
Sandpoint, Idaho

FOREWORD

Since earliest childhood I have had a love affair with America's Frontier West, its music, and history. Many of the songs in this book I recalled from my youth, others have been passed on to me in oral tradition from the old timers that sang them. The songs still fascinate me, many appear in this collection that have never been found in print before.

I have been most fortunate in finding some old time singin' cowboys that shared with me the authentic songs that they sang... and still do! One of my most valuable sources has been the poet-historian, Anthony Wayne Webner, III, whose knowledge and interest of the Old West is reflected in his "traditional-style" poetry.

The drama of the Old West is relived in the strains of these beautiful melodies. The lyrics tell the story of settlers pushing out from Independence and St. Joseph, Missouri, to the far west, and of the dauntless spirit of these pioneers in overcoming the hardships they faced on "the Great American Desert."

They told of their loneliness and longing for loved ones back home in the songs they sang. The cowboys herding the longhorns on the unfenced range sang of little dogies, mules and horses, as well as their sweethearts, and the homes they left behind.

Wherever possible, I have tried to identify the authors of the material used. It is an impossibility to do this consistently as most of these songs were handed down from generation to generation and have been changed from one singing to another. I have collected many of the songs herein, virtually verse by verse over the years, and added a good number of new ones myself as I went along.

It is a pleasure for me to "ride herd" on these songs, poetry, and adages of the past. Proverbs, history, and sayings have been included in my book in the hope that it will give the reader a better understanding of the "way of the Old West."

> *What keeps the herd from runnin',*
> *an' stampedin' far an' wide?*
> *It's the cowboy's long, low whistle,*
> *an' his singin' by their side.*
>
> **- Anon.**

THE SONGS THEY SANG

Out of daily experiences came the songs of the trail and adventure. The long drives gave birth to many a ballad, telling of heroic deeds, or cowboys that went wrong, or a fatal fall from a buckin' bronc. The cowboy's songs tell of carefree daring, of "driving" the dogies, and the quiet solitude of the lonely prairie. Many of the songs he sang were the result of the process of tradition - passing tunes from one person to another, and from one generation to another.

The tunes were hardly ever written down, or standardized. Many changes and variations naturally occurred. These changes often came about as a result of faulty memory on the part of the singer, or from the conscious or unconscious impulse of the cowboy to improve the verse or tune, or maybe to fit the mood of the day!

The purpose of the cowboy's night-herding song was to calm the cattle and keep them from being so easily spooked as they were hard to hold, especially on the first night of the trail drive. The nature of the cowboy's work soon brought about changes in the music that are typically western. Working with cattle inspired shouts and sounds, such as in "The Old Chisholm Trail" and "Git Along Little Dogies."

"The cowboy don't always sing range songs, and many of the old hands sang to tunes imported from the East, when they could get wind of 'em. We sang as much about broken loves as we did about breakin' horses."

- Will James

Many of the western songs began with settlers from the British Isles who brought their fiddles and their music with them to the new land. Stories and songs told of their heritage. "The Streets of Laredo," for example, carries an unchanged Irish melody.

The cowboy gave vent to his emotions by singing about troubles, exhaustion and loneliness. Around the campfire and the occasional ranch party, his spirits were lifted by music that was cheerful and animated. The fiddles played on into the early hours of the morning while friends and neighbors clapped, laughed, danced, drank and forgot their daily struggle for survival.

Originally, the cowboys sang traditional Irish tunes, without accompaniment as they went about their work. They kept many of the old melodies, but changed the words to fit their new surroundings. It is a curious fact that the cowboys learned what has become a part of their tradition from the Swiss yodelers touring the West in the 1880's. The Swiss taught them how to yodel, but the long "drawn out" falsetto, sentimentally sung, is truly a product of the cowboy, and the Mexican vaquero.

The black cowboy enriched American western music as well, with their hollers, blues, spirituals and work songs. After the Civil War, many black Americans came west with their banjos and guitars.

HARMONICALLY, the songs were simple and unsophisticated...
POETICALLY, they were direct, honest, and down to earth...
MUSICALLY, they were a product of the common people...
sprouting up like a tree of "traditional" roots.

In assembling and selecting material for this book, I had the pleasure of meeting and consulting with persons well versed in the tradition of cowboy songs, many of whom were old time working cowboys. I thank them for their friendly assistance, and cooperation.

Personally, I have sung many of the present songs since early childhood. Some are adapted from the singing of my dear mother, who in no small way inspired me musically. Many of the sayings I "inherited" from her.

It is my hope that lovers of authentic American ballads will find these songs of historical, as well as musical, value. History teaches us about our country's past—great events, historic dates, leaders, etc. FOLK stories in SONG and SPEECH reflect the thoughts and feelings of the people.

REMEMBER?
Remember how we gathered 'round
That ol' STOVE in the rear?
The BARBER tellin' stories,
I REMEMBER 'em so clear...
They'd throw ya' in the jailhouse,
If YA' ever told 'em HERE!
- Waldo "Swede" Larson

<u>*FOLK MUSIC DEFINED*</u>: **When FOLKS git together an' ya' HEAR:**
"That ain't the way I heerd it" or *"STOP ME, if you've heerd this before"*, there's FOLK MUSIC bein' made.
-Will McCain Clauson

Index of Songs with Words

Index of Music

Information Index:

Poem Index:

"It was the "hard as steel and tough as nails" cowboy who worked the range and helped settle the early frontier that would later be populated by families migrating west in hope of land and opportunities. Braving the elements, native Indians, wild animals, water shortages, and uncertain employment, they carved a place in history that carries through even into modern times."
-From a gentleman who has been down the road a long ways.

The Cowboy

The cowboy rides through American history as truly a pioneer as the brave and dauntless men who crossed the Appalachians and settled the plains and valleys of our West.

The life of the cowboy, in those days, was both colorful and intense with all of the varied activities; from rounding up the cattle, branding, weaving in and out of the herd, cutting out the fat ones, and riding down bolting steers. At night, they would be riding around the herd to get them huddled and while the night rider stood guard, at last he had time to think and "drink in" the beauties of a roofless world. Or, he might, in soft tones, drawl a yarn to a "compadre," or sing a "hymn" as the two of them stood at their vantage point.

The first American cowboys were Indians, taught by the Spanish missionaries how to ride and herd cattle. The cowboy never would have existed without the horse. Mission Indians and those of mixed blood were called vaqueros (from the Spanish word *vaca* meaning cow). The techniques and skills perfected by these early cow herders spread throughout the West, in addition to their language.

Cowboys roped cattle with a lariat, from the vaquero's *la reata*; chaps, leather trousers worn to protect their legs, is a shortened version of the word *chaparejos*. Other Spanish words that were Anglicized include bronco, cinch, corral, hombre, loco, latigo, remuda and rodeo.

The heyday of the North American cowboy spanned approximately two generations in that brief period of time, the cowhands who rode the cattle trails across the great plains totaled less than fifty thousand. With the invention of the barbed wire in 1874, and an influx of homesteaders who claimed water holes and divided up the range, the old cowboys of the big outfits almost disappeared.

Nearly one third of all cowboys were Mexican or black. The first Anglo American cowboys were primarily Irish, who came west building the Union Pacific Railway, and decided to remain on the frontier. There was an Irish born governor in 1849, and two Irish born senators in 1882.

Two of the wildest towns in the west were Bodie and Aurora, where the wild ways reigned. However, it is interesting to note that you would be much safer strolling around Dodge City in the 1800's than you would be in any major city in the U.S. today. Tombstone had only twenty-five gunmen who "died with their boots on" in the course of a year! The Shamrock Bar in Bodie was where most of the gun fights took place. The sheriff was Irish, as were many of the outlaws, including the Doolin and Dalton gangs.

Between 1846 and 1891, more than three million Irish immigrants came to America. Some 40,000 young Irishmen enlisted to fight in the Indian wars alone, with many more joining the war between the States or to "work upon the railway." General Custer's Seventh Calvary went into battle to the strains of "Garryowen," an old Irish drinking song.

Most of the residents of both Bodie and Aurora were foreign born, the highest percent being Irish, followed by the Chinese (who built the Central Pacific).

Both parents of Billy the Kid were Irish born. The Kidd's real name was Henry McCarty, born in New York in 1859. In the southwest, he became embroiled in a range war between the Murphy, Doolan and Riley gang on one side and the Tunstall and Chisum forces on the other. When things got out of hand, they hired another son of Irish parents, Sheriff Pat Garrett, to hunt him down.

It is said that Garrett caught The Kid at Pete Maxwell's house in New Mexico, where he had hidden out after various killings and a jail break. It is doubtful if there is a more colorful history than that of the Irish in the Old West.

The cowpokes of the 1870's and 80's were hardy young men who labored long hours. Often under wretched conditions, for little pay, in a bone jarring, dangerous occupation. Because most of the cow hunters were so young, they were referred to as cowboys, and the name stuck. Their average age was only twenty-four. As late as the 1920's in the Dakotas it was not unusual for boys as young as eight to be in charge of a herd. They were responsible for the herd's well being and finding grass and water.

The word "cowboy" came from Texas where men would raid Mexican ranches to steal cattle for their coastal stock ranges and to sell in New Orleans. For a time "cowboy" and "cattle rustler" had the same meaning. Men working cattle in the dense brush became known as "brushpoppers." Later, they were called "cowhands" before being known once more as cowboys when cows were moved up the Texas Trail in the 1860's.

The early cowboy rarely owned his own horse. He would however, provide his own saddle, bridle, and rope. Instead of saying that he "worked" a cowboy "rode for" a particular ranch or a brand.

The cowboy ranged from Mexico to the Big Bow River of the north, and from where the trees grew scarce in the East to the Pacific. Besides his horse, all the tools he needed were a saddle, bridle, quirt, hackamore, and a rawhide riata.

The puncher was rigged starting at the top, with a good hat that would protect his head and face from the weather, with maybe a buckskin strap under the chin or behind his head to hold it on. He most often had a big handkerchief tied loose round his neck. In the drag of a trail herd, it was drawn over the face to the eyes "hold up fashion" to protect the nose and throat from dust.

Maybe he'd wear California pants, light buckskin in color with large brown plaid, reinforced with leather, over these came his leggings. His feet were covered with good high heeled boots finished off with steel spurs of Spanish pattern. His weapon was usually a 45 Colt six gun. Sometimes a Winchester in a scabbard was slung to his saddle under his stirrup leather, generally on the left, as his rope hung at the saddle fork on the right. *

In 1888 President Theodore Roosevelt, who ranched for a few years in the Dakota Badlands, described the cowboys as "smaller and less muscular than the wielders of ax and pick, but they are as hardy and self reliant as any men who ever breathed—with bronzed, set faces, and keen eyes that look all the world straight in the face without flinching as they flash out from under their broad - brimmed hats."

Don't take MONEY er PRAISE...
if ya' ain't got it comin'.
-W.M.C

Peril and hardship, and years of long toil, broken by weeks of brutal dissipation, draw haggard lines across their eager faces, but never dim their reckless eyes nor break their bearing of defiant self-confidence.

The cow business in the United States started in Texas and California, and the two states produced two different types of cowpunchers. Those East of the Rockies used saddles with a low horn and double cinch. Their ropes were seldom over forty feet in length, swung with small loops in the bush country. Their chaparejos were made of heavy bull hide to protect their legs from brush and thorns.

The cowboys West of the Rockies, and ranging North, used single cinch saddles with a high fork and cantle, packing a sixty to sixty-five foot rawhide rope. They often used silver mounted spurs, bits and conchas and wore chaparejos made of fur or hair. They called themselves "buckaroos." The Spanish were the first to put brands on their cattle and horses and use the rope.*

There were four major trails over which the cattle were herded north from Texas to railhead towns, such as Cheyenne, Abilene, Kansas and Dodge City, from which they were shipped to the beef hungry cities of the East. Cowhands were also hired as riders to drive the herds of cattle from the Texas ranges to settlements and Army posts in New Mexico, and as far north as Wyoming, Colorado and Idaho.

One of the riskiest, and most strenuous jobs, were the round-ups, held each spring and fall.

The cowboys brought the longhorns in from the range, counted them, and branded the calves born during the year. These were the times of the year that cowboys came drifting in. The cowboys lived in ranch bunk houses, where they ate their meals, swapped stories, and listened to news brought in by the other cowboys.

Waldo Larson, who rode with Rafter A Bar T Ranch, described the bunk house there. "It was thrown together with scrap boards by folks that must have used left handed hammers. It didn't look like much, but the roof kept the rain out and the sides, most of the wind. There was a table, chairs, and an old Ediphone that played 'tubular records,' quite a luxury not found on most ranches! The bunks, eight of them, were just wooden shelves set up above the floor. But after a long hard day's work, who cares?"

Bunk house meals would often consist of a menu of beans, beef, and sourdough bread. At times it would be varied by bacon and eggs, vegetables in season, pies or cake and sweet biscuits called "bannocks."

Many ranches celebrated the beginning of spring roundup with an all night dance, inviting neighbors within a hundred miles radius. For most cowboys, this dance was their main social event of the year. Spring was also the time for the year to round up the horses from their winter range, and prepare the chuck wagon for travel on the range. Spring roundup usually lasted into early summer and when this work was completed, the hands would return to the ranch for repairs and more supplies.

THE GOOD BOOK: Them that reads it have a better chance of doin...what it sez.
-Source: Jim Bottoms

Each summer the beef roundups began. Amid the dust, heat and milling hoofs, the cowboy would weave in and out of the herd cutting out the fat cows and riding down bolting steers. At night the cowboys would stand guard over the herd in two hour shifts, often talking or singing to keep the herd calm.

Andy Adams who worked with the Circle Dot in 1882, stated in his book "the songs which most soothed the cattle were lullabies, ballads, and hymns." During periods of thunderstorms, the cowboys had to be especially alert in the event of a stampede. Sometimes even the striking of a match would be enough to startle the cattle.

When the cowboys were not on the range, there were menial, monotonous, yet essential tasks to be done. On the ranch the cowboy spent his day tending cattle, mending fences, repairing barns, and sheds, taking care of horses and equipment. Sometimes the cowboy even had to milk cows or clean out the chicken coops and stables!

Cowboys only earned $20-$30 per month. Since a new hat might cost one month's wages, he had to choose clothes, boots and hats that were functional and durable.

According to Howard "Chip" Culver, cowboys did not like prairie dogs. They were such a hazard to the horse and rider that a cowboy would often ride many miles to get around a prairie dog town. A prairie dog hole can go straight down as deep as four feet, causing a horse to break its leg if he stepped into it. A prairie dog hole is very distinct, with a collar around it to drain off water when it rains.

U. Utah Phillips has this to say about the long trail drive: "It was worked by a dozen men, two riding on point in front, two on a side four riding swing to keep the herd strung out in a line, and two greenhorns riding drag, the worst job because of the trail dust. There was a wrangler, or a boss wrangler and his crew, because a working cowboy used more than one horse a day. You never ride a horse so much that he gets winded, because then he's no good for anything. You work up a good lather, turn the horse in to the wrangler, and he cuts you out a remount.

"The most important man on the crew is the 'old woman' or the cook. Lots of times a working cowboy wouldn't hire up with the trail drive until he knew who the 'old woman' was, as a spread was often known by its cook. A cowboy's got to make sure he has good grub!"

*(Source Rawhide Rawlins)

When it's stormin' on the prairie,
An' the stock are in corral,
A fella's hardest duty,
Is writin' to his gal.
Source: Aaron Keegan

Folks say "HOWDY",
When yer ridin' HIGH,
When yer DOWN an' OUT,
They'll Pass ya' By.
-Will McCain Clauson

A LETTER FROM DAKOTA

Source:
Raymond W. Ives

New Words and Melody
Will McCain Clauson

A LETTER FROM DAKOTA
(I WANNA COME HOME, BOYS)

I'm writin' you from Deadwood,
Take warnin', boys, from me.
Don't come to the Dakotas,
Ain't nothin' here to see.
Dakota is too cold, boys,
You work six months a year,
And when you go to draw your pay,
There's nothin' left for beer.

Chorus
I wanna come home, boys,
Never to roam, boys,
You can bet your boots and britches,
I'm comin' home.
Don't ever roam, boys,
Stay there at home, boys.
Where the bowlegs stick together,
Way down home.

From Custer up to Deadwood's,
A long and hairy ride,
There's Injuns on the warpath,
Jus' lookin' for your hide.
The Cheyenne and the Sioux, boys,
Will take your duds and hair,
They'll steal your boots and six guns,
And leave you layin' there.

Chorus (repeated)

The Black Hills of Dakota,
Are black as they can be,
With trees so thick and tall, boys,
The hills you cannot see.
The rattlers are so bad, boys,
They're bound to strike your heels,
And leave you for the ki-yotes,
To git a tasty meal.

Chorus (repeated)

The cookie, he cain't cook, boys,
The coffee's black as ink,
The water's full of alkali,
It sure ain't fit to drink.
It's beans, and beef, and biscuits,
You're fed three times a day.
It puts hair on your brisket,
But, ya'd like to run away.

Chorus (repeated)

"Hell's City's" full of muckers,
And choppers walkin' 'round.
They leave no space for bowlegs,
They pushed me outta town.
I'm headin' back fer home, boys,
So pass the word around,
I'll never git consumption,
From sleepin' on the ground.

Chorus (repeated)

bowlegs - cowboys
muckers - miners
choppers - lumberjacks

Some of the words of this song were recalled by Raymond W. Ives (Priest River, Idaho), as sung by his father in Montana.

13

BACKWARDS, TURN BACKWARDS

Lyrics by Anthony Wayne Webner III

Music by Will McCain Clauson

Back-wards, turn back-wards, the page of the book, to the

time of the cow-boy, and take a good look, At the bold and the dash-ing som-

bre-ro clad sons in chaps, spurs, and dus-ters, with blaz-ing six guns.

Back-wards, turn back-wards, the days, boys, _____ to the

Old West of song and re-frain. _____ When our count-ry was young, wild, and

brave, boys, _____ and the Cow-boy was King of the Plain. _____

BACKWARDS, TURN BACKWARDS

Backwards, turn backwards, the page of the book,
To the time of the cowboy and take a good look,
At the bold and the dashing sombrero clad sons,
In chaps, spurs, and dusters, with blazing six guns.
Backwards, turn backwards the days, boys,
To the Old West of song and refrain.
When our country was young, wild, and brave, boys,
And the cowboy was king of the plain.

Cattle

Not long after Columbus sailed to America, Spain became the ruler of Mexico, and other lands to the north. From far across the water the missionaries brought the longhorns. In 1769, the first cattle came to California, and the fertile valley from San Diego to San Francisco became a cowman's paradise. Cattle ran wild and were free for the asking.

Every *vaquero*, (buckaroo) had plenty of cows to call his own, and beef to broil at the campfire. The *Caballeros* (horsemen) became true nobility, who never soiled their hands with humble toil, but living like gentleman, rode around their vast domain, overseeing their laboring peons. It is interesting to note that the term caballero is synonymous with horseman and gentleman in present day Spain.

The southwest climate was so well suited, and the buffalo grass so abundant, that more than three million head of wilderness cattle roamed the grasslands by 1845.

According to Rick Steber the "first real cattle herd brought to the Pacific Northwest was driven overland by mountain man Ewing Young, who formed the Willamette Cattle Company in the fall of 1837, and headed south with nine settlers who had no experience herding cattle. Spending all his money, Young purchased eight hundred Spanish long-horned cattle at the price of three dollars a head, near San Francisco Bay. He had to deny them food and water before they would submit to being driven north."

"When the cattle refused to cross the river at San Joaquin they had to be lassoed one by one and dragged across. The process took one week with a loss of nearly 100 cows drowned. After crossing the Siskiyou mountain range, Young and his drovers arrived in the Willamette Valley with 632 head of cattle. After paying the drovers off in cattle, and keeping a herd for himself, Young sold the remaining cattle at an average of $7.67 a head, becoming the wealthiest man in the area."

Instead of being sent East at the railheads, many of the cattle driven North were bought as stock by ranchers from Kansas, Nebraska, and Colorado, who grazed their herds over thousands of acres of public domain. In turn, those same railheads brought the migration of settlers that claimed these same sections as their own. By 1886 the "open range" had all but disappeared and with it, the long trail drives.

BED DOWN LITTLE DOGIES

Words and Music by
Will McCain Clauson

Slow down, lit – tle do-gies, we've tra – vel'd so

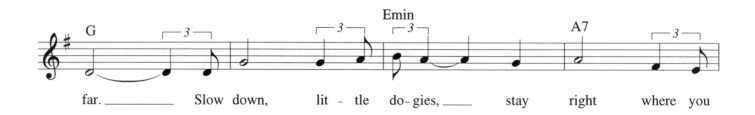

far._____ Slow down, lit – tle do-gies,_____ stay right where you

are. Bed down, lit – tle do-gies,_____ we've got_____ to bed

ground. Don't git_____ so "owl – ey,"_____ quit roam – in' a –

(Guitar)
round.   (Slow)

BED DOWN LITTLE DOGIES

Slow down, little dogies,
We've traveled so far.
Slow down, little dogies,
Stay right where you are.
Bed down, little dogies,
We've got to bed ground.
Don't get so "owley,"
Quit roamin' around.

Slow down, little dogies,
Here's water and feed.
Slow down, little dogies,
Here's all that we need.
Bed down, little dogies,
We've got to bed ground.
Don't get so "owley,"
Quit roamin' around.

The above song is a typical, albeit new version of a night herding song, of which there were many.

BLACK-EYED SUSIE

Traditional Music Arr.
Will McCain Clauson

New Words by
Will McCain Clauson,
Scott & Dianna Reid

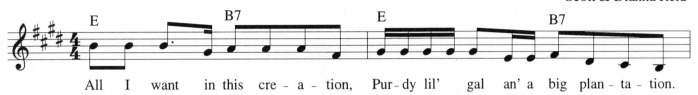

All I want in this cre - a - tion, Pur - dy lil' gal an' a big plan - ta - tion.

Hey! Black- eyed Su - sie Hey, Hey, pur-dy lil' Black-eyed Su - sie Hey!

BLACK-EYED SUSIE

All I want in this creation,
Purdy lil' gal an' a big plantation.

CHORUS:
Hey! Black-eyed Susie.
Hey, hey, purdy lil' black-eyed Susie.
Hey!

All I need to make me happy,
Two lil' boys t'call me pappy.

One called Sop, t'other called Gravy,
One fer the Army, one fer the Navy.

Black-eyed Susie, she's mah daisy,
She's the one that drives me crazy.

Black-eyed Susie, she's a treat,
She's got dimples on 'er feet.

Black-eyed Susie, she's so sweet,
Jus' like sugar on a beet.

Black-eyed Susie, 'bout half grown,
Jump on the boys, like a dawg on a bone!

Two ol' maids sittin' in the sand,
Each of 'em wishin' t'other was a man.

Black-eyed Susie likes to tarry,
She's as tart as huckleberry.

Black-eyed Susie, she's a doozy,
She's my gal an' she's no floozy.

Black-eyed Susie makes me stutter,
I'll take her home to m-m-meet mah Muther.

IRISH PRAYER

May the road rise to meet you,
May the wind be at your back,
May the sun shine warm upon your face,
The rain fall soft upon your fields,
And until we meet again,
May God hold you in the palm of His hand.
-Anonymous

ANOTHER IRISH BLESSING

May there always be work for your hands to do,
May your purse always hold a coin or two.
May the sun always shine on your window pane,
May a rainbow be certain to follow each rain.
May the hand of a friend always be near you,
May God fill your heart with gladness to cheer you.
- Source: Judge Liam DeVally

May you always ride a good horse,
And may you be in Heaven three days
Before the devil knows you're dead!
(A cowboy's paraphrase of the above prayer)

"Settlin' In"

HEALTH

T' git his WEALTH, he spent his HEALTH,
But NUTHIN' did he win,
He turned around an' spent his WEALTH,
To git his HEALTH a-gin.

- Unknown

SETTLIN' IN FER WINTER

Close the door thar, Henry,
It's gittin' cold outside.
Come poke the fire, the Arbuckle's* hot,
It's time to come inside.
You've got the hen coop mended,
The barn's got sweet new hay,
Ol' Bessie's stall is warm 'n snug,
But the sky's turnin' grey.

The pantry's full 'n' bulgin',
The flour's been stowed away,
Sweet cider's jugged 'n' ready,
I've smoked a ham today.
The fruit's bin picked 'n' sorted,
The 'taters packed in sand,
The cannin's done, the cellar's full,
Snow's fallin' 'cross the land.

Fodder's been stacked 'n wood's been split,
Shutters 'r closed fer a while,
The wool's bin spun fer winter clothes,
It's all been done, we kin smile.
I'm startin' on the quiltin', Dear,
New tickin' for the bed,
The still's bin drained fer winter,
An' the jugs are in the shed.

Come sit beside me, Henry,
Put the quilt 'round yer knees,
We'll rock away the winter, Dear,
Pass the jug... would ya' please?

- Dolores Wright

* In the Old West, Arbuckle's brand of coffee was so common it became synonymous with coffee.

FRENCH PHILOSOPHY

A wise man THINKS before he SPEAKS,
A fool SPEAKS before he THINKS,
An' then tries to remember what he said!

-Adapted from a French proverb
-Edited WMC

BUFFALO GALS

Traditional Words and Music
Arranged by Will McCain Clauson

BUFFALO GALS

Buffalo gals, won't ya come out tonight,
Come out tonight, come out tonight?
Buffalo gals, won't ya come out tonight,
An' dance by the light of the moon?

I danced with a gal with a hole in her stockin',
An' her feet kept a'rockin', an' her toe kept a'knockin'
I danced with a gal with a hole in her stockin',
An' we danced by the light of the moon.

Chorus

Won't cha, won't cha, won't cha,
Come out tonight, come out tonight, come out tonight,
Won't cha, won't cha, won't cha,
Come out tonight,
An' dance by the light of the moon.

The Pioneers

They crossed the prairie, as of old
The PILGRIMS crossed the sea,
To make the WEST, as they the EAST,
THE HOMESTEAD OF THE FREE.
-Anon.

The period of Western expansionism saw the molding of a great nation. The Industrial Revolution in the East demanded raw materials from the West. The "Great American Desert" of the plains, as it was called, had to be conquered, and with it the great noblemen of the plain. All in their turn became the children of the "Great White Father," and the way was paved in flesh and blood.

By the mid-1830's the Oregon Trail had opened in the North, and the Santa Fe Trail in the South. This allowed the emigration of huge masses of white settlers to the West. With the popularity of beaver subsiding, the Indian found his popularity with the white man subsiding as well. New avenues of trade were proposed, but the relationship between white man and red was doomed.

"The Great American Treasure Hunt," as Anthony Wayne Webner, III, called it, began in earnest in 1848 in the once Spanish territory of California. Here, at Sutter's Mill, a man found something he wasn't even looking for, at the bottom of a ditch.

The cry of the discovery of gold in this far-off land was heard clear across the continent and around the world, bringing forth the single most influx of white settlers to that state since the coastal settlements of the Russian traders a generation earlier. The race was on.

In a little more than a generation and a half, we would see the destruction of the beaver, the buffalo, the pacification of the Indian, and a war of such ferocious intensity so as to divide family and friend.

Out of the hard simplicity of their lives, out of their vitality, their hopes, their dreams and their sorrows, grew legends of courage and pride. Out of their fever to explore and build, out of the soil enriched by their blood, sprang forth the goods of the earth—great man made lakes, burgeoning agriculture, and thriving industry where once there were burning deserts. Out of their rude settlements and their trading posts came cities to rank among the greatest in the world. The Heritage of a people free to dream, free to act, free to seek, and free to shape their own destiny.

CHOPO

Lyrics by J. Howard Thorpe

Music by Will Clauson

CHOPO

Through rocky arroyos so dark and so deep,
Down hillside or mountain so slippery and steep,
You're brave and you're darin' wherever we go,
And always surefooted, my little Chopo.

Chorus:

Chopo my pony, Chopo my pride,
Chopo "mi amigo," Chopo I ride,
From Mexico's borders cross Texas' "Llanos,"
To the salt Pecos river, I ride you Chopo.

You're a good ropin' horse, you were never jerked down,
When tied to a steer, you will circle him 'round,
Let 'im once cross the string, and it's over he'll go,
You "sabe" the business, my little Chopo.

Repeat Chorus

Whether single or double, or leadin' a team,
Over highways or byways or crossin' a stream,
You're always in fix, and you're rarin' to go,
Whenever you're called on, my little Chopo.

Repeat Chorus

One day on the Llanos a hail storm began,
The cattle stampeded, the horses all ran,
The lightnin' it glittered, a cyclone did blow,
But you faced the sweet music, my little Chopo.

BASSACKWARD TALK

"TARBENDER! TARBENDER!! Pour me a BUBBLE DURBAN fast, I bin bit by a SADDLERAKE," yelled the stranger, runnin' into the saloon.

The Barkeep said, "Slow down, Son, what are ya' talkin' about?"

"I ain't got t-t-time ta t' talk, I gotta have a d-d-drink! I'm t-t-tryin' to tell ya, I bin BIT by a WIDESINDER, an' I'm fast developin' a real bad case of Y-Y-YOURS, I might even be gittin' DRAIN BAMAGED!" he shouted, shakin' all over. "Oh, this YOURS is somethin' TARRIBLE!"

A curious old timer, standin' next to 'im at the bar, asked, "What's YOURS, Son?" The stranger quickly replied, in PERFECT English, "I'll take a DOUBLE BOURBON, thank you!"

He tossed it down, as soon as he got it, an' left sayin', "Keep a LIP UPPER STIFF."

**Old joke-new setting
by Will McCain Clauson**

DEPOT DAY IN WALLACE TOWN

Words and Music by
Will McCain Clauson

Come, ga – ther 'round the sta – tion house on De – pot Day once

more, where gol – den dreams of yes – ter – day still lin – ger as be –

fore. The folks will come from all a – round, they meet here once a

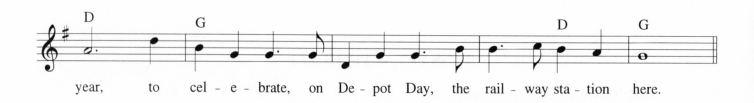

year, to cel – e – brate, on De – pot Day, the rail – way sta – tion here.

Chorus

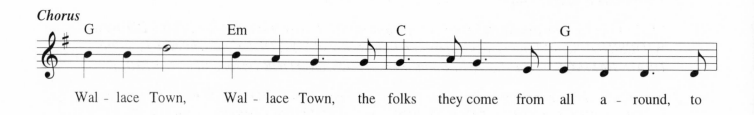

Wal – lace Town, Wal – lace Town, the folks they come from all a – round, to

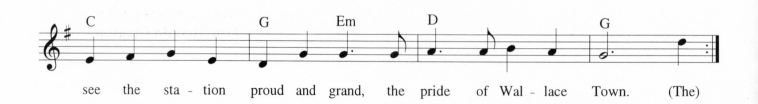

see the sta – tion proud and grand, the pride of Wal – lace Town. (The)

DEPOT DAY IN WALLACE TOWN

Come, gather 'round the station house,
On Depot Day once more.
Where golden dreams of yesterday,
Still linger as before.
The folks will come from all around,
They meet here once a year.
To celebrate on Depot Day,
The railway station here.

Chorus

Wallace Town, Wallace Town,
Folks they come from all around,
To see the station proud and grand,
The pride of Wallace Town!

The wheels of progress told the town,
The station had to go,
We picked it up, and moved it down,
Two hundred feet below.
The Silver Valley station house,
Was built in Nineteen-one.
And still it's standin' proud and grand,
As when the West was young.

Chorus

Wallace Town, Wallace Town,
Folks they come from all around,
To see the station proud and grand,
The pride of Wallace Town!

The trains rolled in, the trains rolled out,
They brought the Mucker's here.
So raise your mugs and give a shout,
And join us in a cheer!
We celebrate the now and then,
The past and future too.
So come along, and join the throng,
We're waitin' here for you.

Chorus

Wallace Town, Wallace Town,
Folks they come from all around,
To see the station proud and grand,
The pride of Wallace Town!

Sweet Rosie at the Jameson,
Will "sit you down" to rest.
Where comfort, cheer, and vittles rare,
Are best in all the West!
If I'm around Two Thousand-one,
If I'm alive and sound,
A big Centennial "Birthday Bash",
I'll see in Wallace Town!

Chorus

Wallace Town, Wallace Town,
Folks they come from all around,
To see the station proud and grand,
The pride of Wallace Town!

LIMERICK

There was an old lady from Nantucket,
She had a bustle as big as a bucket.
She filled it with oats,
And a couple of goats.
They snuck up behind her, and took it.

Folly, ra-lol, Folly, ra-lol,
Folly ra-lol a la louver.
He lifted his hat,
Got hit by a bat,
And he lit on his ear, in the sewer.

-Source: Howard "Chip" Culver

DONEY GAL

New Words by Will McCain Clauson

Trad. Arr. Will McCain Clauson

Chorus:

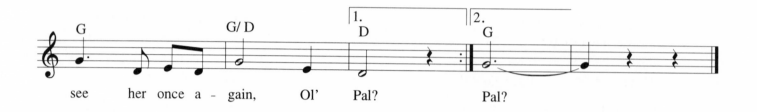

Do - ney Gal, Do - ney Gal, When will I

see her once a - gain, Ol' Pal? Pal?

**Note: Verses have same melody as above Chorus.

DONEY GAL

Drivin' dogies down the trail,
Riding m'Doney Gal in wind or hail,
Rain or shine, sleet or snow,
Me 'n' my Doney Gal are on the go.

Far from home, far from friends,
Sittin' the saddle 'til the trail drive ends.
Longin' for my sweethearts smiles,
Thinkin' of her along the weary miles.

Chorus

Doney Gal, Doney Gal,
When will I see her once again, my Ol' Pal?

KIN YA' HANDLE IT?
It ain't what HAPPENS to ya' that matters,
It's HOW ya' HANDLE it.
- Source: Neil Kennie

TO TOOT OR NOT TO TOOT
He that TOOTETH NOT his own horn;
The same shall not be TOOTED.
- Source: Minnie Gunter

Howard "Chip" Culver

"I began workin' as a cowboy in Nebraska and South Dakota at the ripe ol' age of eight, after the big cattle drives were over, never to return again. Back then, it wasn't unusual for 3,000 or more cattle to be moved for thousands of miles to the rail heads.

"They gave me the nickname 'Chip' 'cause I was always whittlin' as a child, and if I wasn't doing that, I played my mouth harp.

"By the time I started workin' 'em, the cattle drives were not as long and the herd was smaller, usually only two hundred to five hundred head. A typical drive would be from Iowa to South Dakota; or from the eastern end to the mid-west region of the state. The drives were more for findin' good grassland and water for the cows.

"Grassland was abundant then, it was the later plowin' of the land that contributed to the tragic days of the dust bowl. Most of the land was still free range in my day. The few fences on the range were around grain fields, fencin' the grain in and the cattle out.

"Most often a cowboy didn't own more than a saddle, a bridle, and a bedroll. Rarely, if he was lucky, he owned the horse he rode. The horse was usually furnished by the boss and a cowboy used as many as four horses a day on the trail drives. A horse wrangler would take care of the remuda or cavvy, made up of as many as one hundred to two hundred or more horses that would accompany the cattle.

"A cowboy isn't always a cowboy, he often went from job to job, movin' on to other things as needed. Cowboys might at one time be loggers or miners. Miners and loggers, for a time, might be cowboys. One year I supported myself with only an axe, a fiddle and my rifle. I only worked a few years breakin' horses. Most of us cowboys soon got out of it because of the fear of broken bones and the many sorts of injuries that could and did happen.

"The trail boss would usually 'eye' your bedroll, if it looked good, you'd stand a chance of gettin' hired. We carried everything we needed on the trail in the bedroll, and once we got goin' it would be carried in the chuck wagon. We slept under the open sky and hardly ever sat down on a chair. We used the squattin' position when we rested, we'd always take our spurs off first!

"Cowboys sang some, but more often just talked to their mounts or dogies. Their job was to keep the cows movin', the singin' was just incidental. Fortunately, it so happened that I was blessed with a good singin' voice, and I confess, I did sing some to 'em.

"My Aunt Katie would ask neighbors over and I'd perform for them. I didn't have an accordion at that time so I sang a capella (that means you ain't got enough cash to buy a squeeze box!). Anyhow, the folks liked to hear the songs, and I liked to sing 'em. I finally got a button accordion and started playin' for dances.

"My grandpa and dad had a road construction outfit. They had as many as eighty head of horses, and hired many men. When I worked with my dad we lived in 'road shacks' that were eight feet by sixteen. They were pulled by horses from job to job. We had to withstand the heat of cooking indoors because there were too many flies outside.

"I later went to New Mexico as a surveyor, right on the Mexican border. There were no roads. The men lived in bunkhouses, we had three of 'em: one for surveyors, one for well drillers, and one for the cowboys. They butchered two steers a week to feed the crew. We had beef, beans, and biscuits...three times a day. Always the same...the cooks did the best they could with what they had.

"After I quit cowboyin', I worked in South Dakota as a forest ranger on Harney Peak, as lookout. While there, the great cowboy poet Charles 'Badger' Clark, the Poet Laureate of South Dakota, came to visit me. He'd call himself Poet "Lariat!" I'd git a fire going in a pit that I'd made out of stone, with a fine seatin' arrangement. There we would sit around the camp fire 'swappin' songs.' He would borrow my guitar, sing a song, an' pass it on to me. Then I'd sing one of mine for him. He was a great singer and story teller as well as a poet. I'm proud to have known him.

"It was different livin' in the Midwest than it was out further. Over the Rocky Mountains you didn't have the open range and cattle drives so much. They had small ranches, an' a little of everything: a few cows to milk, a few chickens, a pig or two, maybe sheep. They grew their own food in the garden, had fruit from the orchard and berries from the patches.

"One thing they didn't have was money, but they ate well, most of the time. It was a peaceful, quiet life. Folks seemed to be happy with simple pleasures."

EATIN' GOOBER PEAS

Composed by P. Nutt

Arranged by Will McCain Clauson

EATIN' GOOBER PEAS

Sittin' by the roadside on a summer day
Chattin' with my mess mates, passin' time away.
Lyin' in the shadow underneath the trees.
Goodness, how delicious, eatin' goober peas.

Chorus
Peas! Peas! Peas! Peas!
Eatin' goober peas!
Goodness how delicious.
Eatin' goober peas!

When the horseman passes, the soldiers have a rule.
To cry out at their loudest, "Mister, here's your mule."
But another pleasure enchantinger than these.
Is wearin' out your grinders eatin' goober peas.

Chorus
Peas! Peas! Peas! Peas!
Eatin' goober peas!
Goodness how delicious.
Eatin' goober peas!

Just before the battle, the gen'ral hears a row.
He says, "The Yanks are comin', hear their rifles now."
He turns around in wonder, whatcha think he sees?
A band of Georgia soldiers eatin' goober peas.

Chorus
Peas! Peas! Peas! Peas!
Eatin' goober peas!
Goodness how delicious.
Eatin' goober peas!

Now my song has lasted almost long enough.
The subject's interestin', but rhymes are mighty rough.
When this war is over, and free from rags and fleas,
We'll kiss our wives and sweethearts and gobble goober peas.

Chorus
Peas! Peas! Peas! Peas!
Eatin' goober peas!
Goodness how delicious.
Eatin' goober peas!

The composer ot this popular Civil War song is P. Nutt and that's what goober peas are (peanuts). Whoever wrote it had a good sense of humor, as shown in the words and the cheerful melody. Many a Civil War soldier later brought the song with them out west, where it was sung around the cowboy campfires.

GIT ALONG LITTLE DOGIES

Traditional Arranged and Adapted by
Will McCain Clauson

As I was a - rid - in' one mor - nin' fer pleas - ure, I

spied a cow - punch - er a - rid - in' a - long. His

hat was throwed back and his spurs was a - jing - lin', an'

as he ap - proached he was sing - in' this song. Whoo-pee

Ti - Yi - Yo_____ Git a - long, lit - tle dog - ies, _____

it's your mis - for - tune __ an' none of my own. Whoo-pee

Ti - Yi - Yo, Git a - long, lit - tle do - gies. Ya'

know that Wy - o - min' will be yer new home. (Guitar solo line to end)

GIT ALONG LITTLE DOGIES

As I was a ridin' one mornin' for pleasure,
I spied a cow puncher a ridin' along.
His hat was throwed back and his spurs was a jinglin',
And as he approached he was singin' this song.

Chorus
Whoopee Ti Yi Yo, Git along little dogies,
It's your misfortune an' none of my own.
Whoopee Ti Yi Yo, Git along little dogies,
Y' know that Wvomin' will be yer new home.

It's early in spring that we round up the dogies,
We mark 'em an' brand em', an' bob off their tails.
We round up the hosses, load up the chuck wagon,
An' then throw the dogies out into the trail.

Chorus
Whoopee Ti Yi Yo, Git along little dogies,
It's your misfortune an' none of my own.
Whoopee Ti Yi Yo, Git along little dogies,
Y' know that Wvomin' will be yer new home.

Yer mama was born away down in Texas,
Where the jimson weed and sandburrs grow.
We'll fatten ya' up, when we git to Wyomin',
An' then move ya' on to Idaho.

Chorus
Whoopee Ti Yi Yo, Git along little dogies,
It's your misfortune an' none of my own.
Whoopee Ti Yi Yo, Git along little dogies,
Y' know that Wvomin' will be yer new home.

Cowboys did not "bob off" dogie tails. The unknown poet could have been a former sheep man looking for a word to rhyme with trail, or could be a "polite" reference to castration.

Alternate line: "We mark 'em and brand 'em, and foller their tails."

HURRAHIN' UP THE TOWN

The boys are ridin' in t'night,
They're shootin' up the town.
The rustlers are on the trail,
An' the Sheriff's boggin' down.

The Palace Bar is lighted,
The waddies are rarin' t' go.
The gamblers, in their spotless shirts,
Will be rakin' in the dough.
- Anon., -Circa 1870

GIT ALONG HOME, CINDY

Traditional Arr. Will McCain Clauson

New Words by Will McCain Clauson

You ought to see my Cin - dy, She lives a - way down South. She's so sweet the hon – ey bees buzz a - round her mouth. Git a - long home, home, Cin - dy, Git a - long home, home, Cin - dy, Git a - long home, home, Cin - dy, You'll be mine some - day.

GIT ALONG HOME, CINDY

You ought to see my Cindy,
She lives away down South.
She' s so sweet the honey bees
Buzz around her mouth.

Chorus
Git along home, home, Cindy.
Git along home, home, Cindy.
Git along home, home Cindy
You'll be mine some day.

Her lips are like a cherry.
Her cheeks are like a rose.
How I love that sassy gal,
Most everybody knows.

Chorus

I wish I had a nickel,
I wish I had a dime,
I wish I had my Cindy here,
I'd love her all the time.

Chorus

I wish I had an apple,
A-hangin' on a tree.
Then ev'ry time my Cindy passed,
She'd take a bite of me.

Chorus

You never know with Cindy,
How things are gonna be.
Jes' when you think you got her down,
She's gotcha up a tree.

Chorus

She told me that she loved me.
She called me sugar plum.
She threw her arms around my neck.
I thought my time had come

Chorus

I never think of Cindy,
That I don't think of sin.
I'm always knockin' at her door,
But she don't let me in.

Chorus

My Cindy got religion.
She had it once before.
But when she hears my ol' banjo,
She's first upon the floor.

Chorus

Some day I'll marry Cindy,
She's ev'ry thing I've said.
I'll love her 'til the day I died,
I'll love her 'til I'm dead.

Chorus

We'll make ourselves a baby,
I hope it looks like me.
And if it don't I'll sail away,
And jump into the sea.

Chorus

This is another southern dance tune that found its way to the west. I took the liberty of adding a few new verses (not that the song needed them). See if you can guess which ones are new.

TO SPEAK OR NOT TO SPEAK
(The Wise Old Owl)

*A wise old owl sat in an oak,
the MORE he saw, the LESS he spoke.
The LESS he spoke, the MORE he heard,
Why can't WE be like that wise old bird?*
- Source: Waldo "Swede" Larson

GOIN' HOME
A Cowboy Gospel Song

Words and Music by
Will McCain Clauson

Oh, I'm rid-in' 'cross the plains to way up yon - der, To my
fin - al rest, I will go. Though the
trail is steep an' rock - y as I wan - der, From a
sin - ful world be - low.

Chorus

I'm go - in'
home, _____ go - in' home, _____
Home to one last round - up in the sky. I'm go - in'
home, _____ go - in' home, _____
Round - ed up in glo - ry by an' by. _____

GOIN' HOME
(A Cowboy Gospel Song)

Oh, I'm ridin' 'cross the plains to way up yonder,
To my final rest, I will go
'Though the trail is steep and rocky as I wander,
From a sinful world below.

Chorus
I'm goin' home, goin' home,
Home to one last roundup in the sky.
I'm goin' home, goin' home,
Rounded up in Glory, bye an' bye.

Oh, I'm headin' up the trail and 'cross the water,
To a bright an' golden shore.
Where the dark and stormy clouds will never gather,
We shall meet to part no more.

Chorus
I'm goin' home, goin' home,
Home to one last roundup in the sky.
I'm goin' home, goin' home,
Rounded up in Glory, bye an' bye.

Up on high, His gentle voice I'll soon be hearin',
As the Herder takes me home.
Oh, I know the last big roundup soon is nearin',
In His pasture I will roam.

Chorus
I'm goin' home, goin' home,
Home to one last roundup in the sky.
I'm goin' home, goin' home,
Rounded up in Glory, bye an' bye.

A great deal of emphasis has been placed on the lawless aspects of the old west. The circuit riding preacher was not uncommon, and the cowboys did indeed sing hymns and contemplated "The Great Beyond." In their solitude they had lots of time to sing the songs they wrote and pass them on in oral tradition: songs like "Last Night As I Lay on the Prairie," "The Night Herder's Lament," "We'll Be Rounded Up In Glory," etc.

WORK	SLICK ADVICE
We go t'WORK,	*"All things come to him who waits,*
T'earn the DOUGH,	*But here's a rule that's SLICKER,*
T'buy the BREAD,	*The man who GOES fer what he wants*
T'git the STRENGTH,	*WILL GIT IT ALL THE QUICKER!"*
T'GO T'WORK.	
- Unknown - Edited W M C	**- Unknown - Edited W M C**

GOOD-BYE OL' PAINT

Trad. Music Arranged by
Will McCain Clauson

New Words by
Anthony Wayne Webner III

Good - bye, Ol' Paint, I'm lea - vin' Chey -
enne. Good - bye Ol' Paint, I'm leav - in' Chey -
enne. I'm leav - in' Chey - enne, I'm off to Mon - tan', Good -
bye, Ol' Paint, I'm leav - in' Chey - enne. _____

GOOD-BYE, OL' PAINT

Good-bye, Ol' Paint, I'm leavin' Cheyenne,
Good-bye, Ol' Paint, I'm leavin' Cheyenne.

I'm leavin' Cheyenne, I'm off to Montan',
Good-bye, Ol' Paint, I'm leavin' Cheyenne.

You've been a good pony, you've been a good friend,
But all things change, and come to an end.

I'm drivin' the stage coach alone on this run,
My cow punchin' days are over and done.

My boot's on the brake, the line's in my hand,
The coach is packed, the hitch they won't stand.

I'm settin' you free, boy, to run with the wind,
Good-bye, Ol' Paint, my faithful old friend.

With whip crack, and whistle, the leads take the lines,
Good-bye to Ol' Paint, Good-bye to old times.

HATS OFF TO THE COWBOY

Words by Waldo "Swede" Larson

Music by Will McCain Clauson

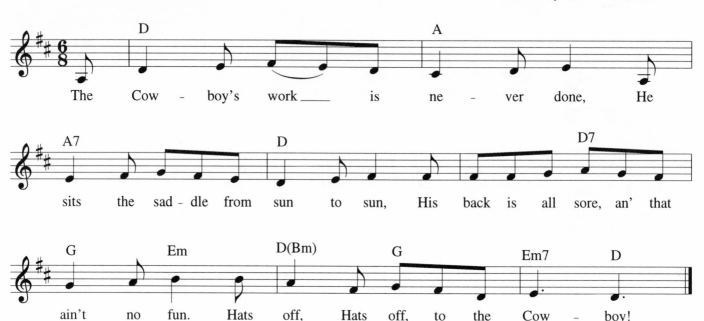

HATS OFF TO THE COWBOY!

The Cowboy's work is never done,
He sits the saddle from sun to sun.
His back is all sore, an' that ain't no fun.
HATS OFF! HATS OFF TO THE COWBOY!

He never complains when the goin' gets rough,
He punches fer wages that ain't near enough.
An' his easiest job is purdy durn tough.
HATS OFF! HATS OFF TO THE COWBOY!

He don't like t'walk, he wuz born on a horse,
An' sometimes his "lingo" gits a little bit "corse."
Sometimes it's good, but mostly it's worse.
HATS OFF! HATS OFF TO THE COWBOY!

He'll clean out the stalls, he'll help out the cook,
He'll even slop hogs, if the job ain't been took.
He'll even herd sheep if there's no one t'look.
HATS OFF! HATS OFF TO THE COWBOY!

His rowles are worn to a nubbin' or worse,
From ridin' the "hurricane deck of a horse,"
He'll met the "Big Tally" with boots on, o'corse.
HATS OFF! HATS OFF TO THE COWBOY!

He'll git into town when the work is all done,
To meet with the ladies, and have 'im some fun.
At stompin' "cotillion," he's "A" Number One.
HATS OFF! HATS OFF TO THE COWBOY!

He'll never back down in a barroom fight,
He'll kick up his heels on a Saturday night,
An' toss down a few, when the feelin' is right.
HATS OFF! HATS OFF TO THE COWBOY!

HATS OFF TO THE COWBOY! He helped win the West.
HATS OFF TO THE COWBOY! He's always the best.
HATS OFF TO THE COWBOY! With hair on his chest.
HATS OFF! HATS OFF TO THE COWBOY!!

The Civil War

JUST BEFORE THE BATTLE, MOTHER,
I am thinking most of you,
While up on the field we're watching,
With the enemy in view.
Comrades, brave are 'round me lying,
Filled with thoughts of home and God,
For well they know that on the morrow,
Some will sleep beneath the sod.
- George F. Root, 1862

The Civil War began on April 13, 1861, when Major Robert Anderson surrendered the Union fort at Fort Sumter, standing in Charleston Harbor, South Carolina. Confederate batteries had fired on the embankments the previous day. During the Civil War, about 60% of the Union Army and about 30% of the Confederate Army were Irish, or of Irish decent.

One of the bloodiest battles of the War between the States occurred on September 19 and 20, 1863. The Confederates, led by General Braxton Bragg defeated the Federal troops. Combined losses out of the 125,000 men involved totaled 34,000 men.

Other notable battles included Chalmette, Louisiana, on December 28, 1814, during which the British were driven back after severe fighting against troops commanded by Andrew Jackson. General Johnston, with his 60,000 Confederates, held their ground against General Sherman and his 100,000 Federal troops in a battle that lasted for several weeks in June, 1864, at Kenesaw Mountain, Georgia. Confederate General Polk was killed here before his troops were forced to retire after several heavy engagements.

Appomattox, Virginia, was the site of the final battle on April 8, 1865, when General Lee surrendered his 35,000 men to General Grant and his troops of 100,000 men. One of the most bitter wars ever fought was over and the Union was saved.

After the surrender of Lee to Grant, the soldiers of the latter, began, without orders, to salute Grant with cannon. He directed the firing to cease, lest it should WOUND the feelings of the prisoners, who, he said, were still THEIR COUNTRYMEN.

"Yankee" and "Rebel" tunes, sung during this dramatic period became very popular. Some of them, like the one above, were sung by both sides. They spoke of battle campaigns and abolitionists; they were inspirational tunes, marching songs and patriotic hymns. They were later to be sung by many a cowboy, who also sang the popular songs of the day.

They are a significant part of our National musical heritage: "The Battle Cry of Freedom," "Battle Hymn of the Republic," "Dixie Land," and "When Johnny Comes Marching Home." "The Yellow Rose of Texas" and "Goober Peas" are included in the book.

With malice toward none, with charity for all, with firmness in the right as God gives us to see the right, let us strive on.

-Abraham Lincoln

HELL-BOUND FREIGHT

Words by Anthony Wayne Webner III

Music by Will McCain Clauson

On a stor - min' night that was black an' cold, near the

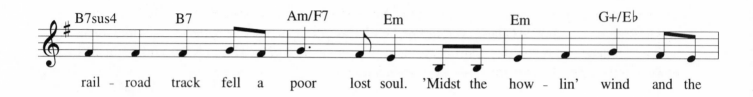

rail - road track fell a poor lost soul. 'Midst the how - lin' wind and the

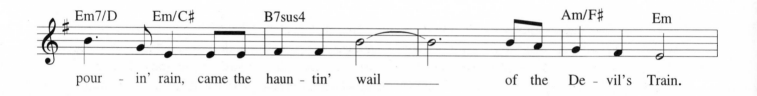

pour - in' rain, came the haun - tin' wail_____ of the De - vil's Train.

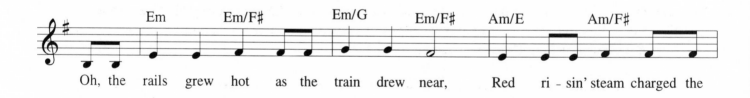

Oh, the rails grew hot as the train drew near, Red ri - sin' steam charged the

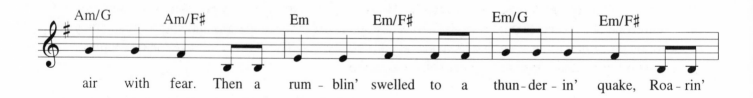

air with fear. Then a rum - blin' swelled to a thun - der - in' quake, Roa - rin'

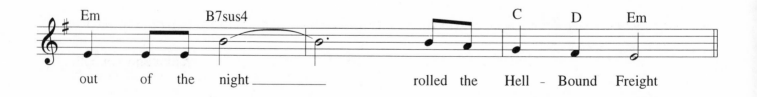

out of the night_____ rolled the Hell - Bound Freight

HELL-BOUND FREIGHT

On a stormin' night that was black and cold,
Near the railroad tracks fell a poor lost soul.
'Midst the howlin' wind and the pourin' rain,
Came the hauntin' wail of the Devil's Train.
Oh, the rails grew hot as the train drew near,
Red risin' steam charged the air with fear.
Then a rumblin' swelled to a thunderin' quake,
Roarin' out of the night rolled the Hell-Bound Freight.

Chorus
When the Hell-Bound Freight's a rollin',
Lightnin' flashes, thunder peals,
As the Devil's blood black engine roars,
Down the tracks of brimstone steel.
O'er the din of sinners dyin',
O'er the banshee whistle blast,
Hear Ol' Satan call the stations,
As the freight goes roarin' past.
"Now, it's all aboard for Limbo,
Purgatory's next, my friends,
Cross the bridge at 'Lake 'a' Fire,'
Hell's a-waitin' 'round the bend.
Oh, this Hell-On-Wheel's a-rollin',
'Cause Perdition just won't wait."
Ya' better mend your ways, you sinners,
Or you'll ride the Hell-Bound Freight.

The damned, they were jam-packed in stockyard cars,
A-reachin' and screechin' through the slats and bars,
They bellered for mercy, they bawled and squealed,
Like slaughterhouse stock, oh, their doom was sealed.
There were rich men, poor men, beggars and thieves,
There was every faith, there was all beliefs,
All colors and hues, every shape and size,
Oh, the whole damned world passed before his eyes.

Chorus

As the last doomed car went rattlin' by,
Oh, the poor lost soul heard a piercin' cry.
Through the box car slats, from a tortured space,
The sinner man saw his own damned face.
"O Sinner Man where ya' gonna run to?
O Sinner Man where ya' gonna run to?
O Sinner Man where ya' gonna run to?
All on that day!"
The sinner man woke with a piercin' scream,
Sweatin' and shakin' from his Hell-Bound Dream.
On his knees he prayed, "Say it ain't too late...,"
"Oh, save me Lord, from the Hell-Bound Freight."

Chorus

HER LOVE WAS A BUSTER

Words Adapted by W M C
From a poem by Belle Starr

Trad. Music Arr. by
Will McCain Clauson

HER LOVE WAS A BUSTER

Her love was a buster, wild broncos he'd break,
He promised he'd quit it, an' all for her sake.
One foot he tied up, an' the saddle throwed on,
With a jump an' a holler, he was mounted an' gone.

The first time she saw him was early one spring,
A-ridin' a bronco, a strong-headed thing.
Oh, she was so smitten, she let out a sigh,
As he tipped her a wink, but he passed her on by,

The next time she saw him was late in the fall,
A-swingin' them ladies at the ro-de-o ball.
He laughed, an' he talked as they swung to an' fro,
An' he promised he'd quit ridin' buckin' broncos.

He gave her some presents, among them a ring,
What she gave in return was a far better thing.
The young maiden's heart, I'll have you to know,
Was won by the man on the buckin' bronco.

But he still got his gun, an' the gun he can use,
He ain't quit gunfightin', an' he ain't quit the booze.
He still sits the saddle, he still swings the rope,
He ain't quit cowpunchin' the way that she hoped.

Now all you young ladies, where'er you reside,
Beware of them busters that swing the rawhide.
They'll court ya', an' pet ya', then leave ya' an' go,
Up the trail in the spring, to the buckin' bronco.

43

HOME ON HIGH

Source: Howard "Chip" Culver

New Words and Music
Will McCain Clauson

To - night I'm a poor wear-y cow - boy, _____ I've

been in the sad - dle all day, _____ Out

search - in' the hills and the val - leys, _____ For

cat - tle ____ that strayed _____ a - way. _____ Ol'

Paint is so worn out and tired, _____ His

feet are bro - ken and sore. _____ But

when the trail drive is o - ver, _____ We'll _

ride on that oth - er ____ shore. _____

HOME ON HIGH

Tonight I'm a poor weary cowboy,
I've been in the saddle all day,
Out searchin' the hills and the valleys,
For cattle that strayed away,
Old Paint's so worn out and tired,
His feet are broken and sore,
But when the "trail drive" is over,
We'll ride on that other shore.

Sometimes when the dogies are sleepin',
On my saddle I pillow my head,
And up at the heaven's lie peepin',
From out of my cold, grass bed.
It's out on the prairie I wonder,
At night while lying alone,
On one of them bright stars up yonder,
Could a poor cowboy's soul find home?

They say there's to be a great roundup,
Where cowboys like dogies will stand,
To be cut out by riders of judgement,
Who are posted and know ev'ry brand,
Tonight as I lay on the prairie,
And look at the stars in the sky,
I wonder if ever a cowboy,
Would drift to that home on high.

Tonight as the bright stars are twinklin'
like diamonds set up in the sky,
I find myself lying and thinkin'
That maybe God's heav'n is nigh.
I wonder if there I shall meet her,
My mother that God took away.
If there in His kingdom I'll greet her
Up there on the last round up day.

The trail to the great mystic region,
Is narrow and dim, so they say,
The one that leads down to perdition
Is posted and blazed all the way.
I'm 'fraid I'll be a stray yearlin',
A maverick unbranded on high,
Drug 'way in the bunch with the "rusties,"
When the Boss of the Riders goes by.

If the gate should be open up yonder,
I'll whistle so soft and so low,
And then Old Paint will come runnin',
From a far distant pasture I know.
I'll give him a handful of sugar,
I'll watch him say "Thanks" with his eyes.
I'll mount and we'll ride across the prairie,
And report to the Boss on high.

This is a composite cowboy song with many authors, including myself. Parts of it saw the light in 1898. It has been known as "Roll On, Little Dogies," "The Cowboy's Dream" and "A Cowboy's Reverie." The latter was sung to me by Howard "Chip" Culver, who said the composer of the music was unknown to him.

HOME ON THE RANGE

Words by Dr. Bruce Higley
Traditional Cowboy Song

Music by Daniel Kelley
Arr. by Will McCain Clauson

HOME ON THE RANGE

Oh, give me a home where the buffalo roam,
Where the deer and the antelope play.
Where seldom is heard a discouragin' word,
An' the skies are not cloudy all day.

Chorus
Home, home on the range,
Where the deer and the antelope play,
Where seldom is heard a discouragin' word,
An' the skies are not cloudy all day.

How often at night when the heavens are bright,
With the light from the glitterin' stars,
Have I stood there amazed and asked as I gazed,
If their glory exceeds that of ours.

Chorus

Where the air is so pure and the zephyrs so free,
And the breezes so balmy and light.
Oh, I would not exchange my home on the range,
For all of your cities so bright.

Chorus

Words were written by Dr. Bruce Higley of Ohio in 1873, and were published as a poem entitled "My Western Home." Daniel Kelley later composed the melody, which still lacked the title "Home on the Range." The cowboys out West took care of that part of the song, and wrote a chorus for it. Also, the words here are almost identical to one version printed in 1910.

MONEY

*Money buys fried eggs an' sausage,
'Nuff "red eye" to fill up yer pot.
When ya've got lots o' money,
Ya' feel kinda funny,
An' the gals seem to like ya' a lot.*

*The gals in Dodge City all know me,
They all like to tickle my toes.
I give 'em some money,
They all call me "Honey,"
'n start takin' off all my clothes.*

*They don't have to tickle my fancy,
If they do, it's a real special treat.
But it ain't very funny,
When they take all yer money,
An' don't even tickle yer feet!*

*Money's like beer in yer bucket,
Money's like juice in yer jar.
Ya' drink up yer money,
Get boozey an' funny,
An' wake up with yer head on the bar!*
- Will McCain Clauson

THE STAMPEDE

When the hot sun smiles,
On the endless miles,
That lead to the distant mart,
And the cattle wail,
Down the well-worn trail,
And moan till it grips the heart,
And they gasp for air,
In the dust clouds there,
As they jostle their way along,
With uplifted ear,
So that they may hear,
The cow-puncher's evenin' song.

Far up at the head,
Rode Ol' Texas Red,
A man of determined face—
And his keen grey eye,
Took in earth and sky,
As he rode with a *centaur's grace.
On the left was Joe,
On his lil' pinto,
Jim Smith patrolled on the right.
We were numbered ten,
All were needed then,
As we rode that fateful night.

To quench our thirst,
We had dared the worst,
And fought for a nester's well;
But he had a girl,
With a witchin' curl,
And she cast a golden spell.
So our shots went wide,
From the sinner's hide,
As he faded from our view.
And the charmin' miss,
Blew Ol' Red a kiss,
And smiled as his pony flew.

'Twas a pretty play,
But he spurred away,
His face like a prairie blaze.
And he hit the dirt,
As he plied his quirt,
Till lost in the frenzied haze,
While the bawlin' shrilled,
As the cattle milled,
And their eyes grew shot with fear-
For they knew right well,
That a merry hell,
Lurked in the gatherin' smear.

In the north black clouds,
Like funeral shrouds,
Rolled down with an icy breath,
And we faced a fight,
On a brutal night,
With odds on the side of death.
For a trailin' herd,
When it's rightly stirred
Is a thing for a man to shun.
And no coward band,
Ever holds command,
When the norther's on the run.

In the ghostly hush,
That precedes the rush,
Of the wild wind-driven flood,
We made our dash,
To the thunder's crash,
Spurs set till they drew the blood;
But the Storm King struck,
To our bitter luck,
We rode in the lightnin's glare.
And the north wind whirled,
Through a watery world,
And laughed at our puny dare.

There was death at stake,
And 'twas make or break,
In the rush of that frenzied mob;
But we'd risked our lives,
In a hundred drives,
And we figured to know our job.
Then a sudden hail,
On the whistlin' gale
And a horse went slitherin' by—
'Twas Ol' Texas Red,
And we knew he sped,
To the girl of the flashin' eye.

With a wicked grip,
On his bitin' whip,
He raced in on the heavin' ranks,
And his searchin' eye,
Set to do or die,
As he fanned at his pony's flanks;
And we gazed aghast,
When we saw at last—
Ol' Tex at the head of the ruck,
And we made a prayer,
For the rider there,
Just a wish for a hero's luck.

Straight she stood and still,
At the storm's wild will,
Close by the nester's well,
And her eyes were kissed,
By the drivin' mist,
As she faced that livin' hell,
But when Texas Red,
'crost his pony's head,
Erect in his stirrups rose,
Like a sprite she sprung
—to his shoulder clung—
A rod from the leader's nose.

'Twas a gallant race,
But he held his pace,
As he edged to the leeward side.
Not a moment's slip,
Of his strong arm's grip,
As he led that bawlin' tide;
And his noble steed,
Knowin' well the need,
Gave of his stout heart's best,
And he brought them free,
From that maddened spree,
And slid—in the mud—to rest.

Yes, we found the two,
Where the north wind blew,
Her black hair across his breast;
In his arms she clung,
As his big heart sung,
Under his calfskin vest.
And the lucky brute,
Made us each salute,
And she kissed us one by one,
And we all went wild,
Till Ol' Tex got riled,
And threatened to pull a gun.

On the trail we lay,
At the break of day,
Deep in the Texas mud—
Dog-tired we dragged,
As the cattle lagged,
Coolin' their racin' blood;
'Twas a weary trek,
To the river's neck,
And we longed for the scorchin' sun,
And we drank to Red's luck,
As we downed our chuck,
And we sang—for the night was done!

Source: Yardley

Edited: Clauson

*Centaur: Greek mythical beast, half man and half horse.

It pleases me to be able to present this dramatic creation by an anonymous poet of the past. It is by far, in my opinion, the finest example of Western classic poetry that I have found.

*This page has been
left blank to avoid
awkward page turns*

IN IDAHO

New Words by
Will McCain Clauson

Traditional Music
Arr. & Adapt. Will Clauson

Where North-ern skies still touch the West, And prai - ries rise to moun-tain

crest, There is a land that's tru - ly blessed, ___ it's I - DA - HO.

IN IDAHO

Where Northern skies still touch the West,
And prairies rise to mountain crest,
There is a land that's truly blessed — it's IDAHO.

Where ring necked pheasant flush and fly,
Where salmon charge white rapids high,
And soaring eagles dot the sky — in IDAHO.

Where, far beneath the bighorn sheep,
Perched high on craggy granite steep,
The cattle graze in meadows deep — in IDAHO.

The bear and wolf still forage there,
In leafy glen browse white tail deer,
The mountain bluebird you will hear — in IDAHO.

The Indian proud, the mountaineers,
The lonely trappers, pioneers
Those were the men who ventured here — to IDAHO.

Where sunrise paints the timberline,
And colors gleam through larch and pine.
Syringa bloom come summertime — in IDAHO.

A land of crystal lakes and streams,
The land I searched for in my dreams
A paradise I found it seems, — in IDAHO.

Syringa — state flower   Mountain bluebird — state bird

Eight lines of the above poem were inscribed on an old time wallhanger. I took the liberty of expanding upon the unknown author's theme.

I dedicate this song to the pioneering spirit of the Idahoan, and to the land of my forefathers who settled there over 100 years ago in the Silver Valley. I now reside in the Idaho Panhandle, an area that I dearly love.

IN THE PALM OF HIS HAND

Words & Music Will Clauson

May God lead you, in the Spi-rit of His love, May God
There is Hea-ling in the Pow-er of His hand, There is

lead you, in the Spi-rit of His love, May God
Hea-ling in the Pow-er of His hand, There is

lead you in the Spi-rit of His love. Hal-le-
Hea-ling in the Pow-er of His

lu-jah! In the Spi-rit of His love,

May God hold you in the palm of His hand, May God

hold you in the palm of His hand, May God

hold you in the palm of His hand, Hal-le-

lu-jah, in the palm of His hand.

IN THE PALM OF HIS HAND

May God lead you in the spirit of His love,
(Repeat two more times)
Hal - le - lu - jah, in the spirit of His love.

There is healing in the power of His hand,
(Repeat two more times)
Hal - le - lu - jah, in the power of His hand.

Chorus:
May God hold you in the palm of His hand,
(Repeat two more times)
Hal - le - lu - jah, in the palm of His hand.

There is freedom from the chains of sin.
(Repeat two more times)
Hal - le - lu - jah, from the chains of sin.

Sweet salvation, from the gift of His hand.
(Repeat two more times)
Hal - le - lu - jah, from the gift of his hand.

Chorus

Praise and glory to the Savior and the King,
(Repeat two more times)
Hal - le - lu - jah, from the gift of His hand.

Let his light shine, all around this land
(Repeat two more times)
Hal - le - lu - jah, all around this land.

Spread the good news, all over this world,
(Repeat two more times)
Hal - le - lu - jah, all around this land.

Chorus

The words to the fifth verse were written by Pastor Dennis Hanson, of the First Lutheran Church in Sandpoint, Idaho.

While living in Europe in the early '50's, I had the pleasure of first recording one of my gospel songs, "He's Got the Whole World in His Hand." It was later passed on in the oral folk song tradition, and became a world wide hit. The above is another gospel song composed to glorify His name.

---

*"It ain't the FINAL score that counts,
It's the WAY ya' PLAY the GAME."*

- Source: Waldo "Swede" Larson

I'VE BEEN WUKKIN' ON THE RAILROAD

Traditional

Arranged by Will McCain Clauson

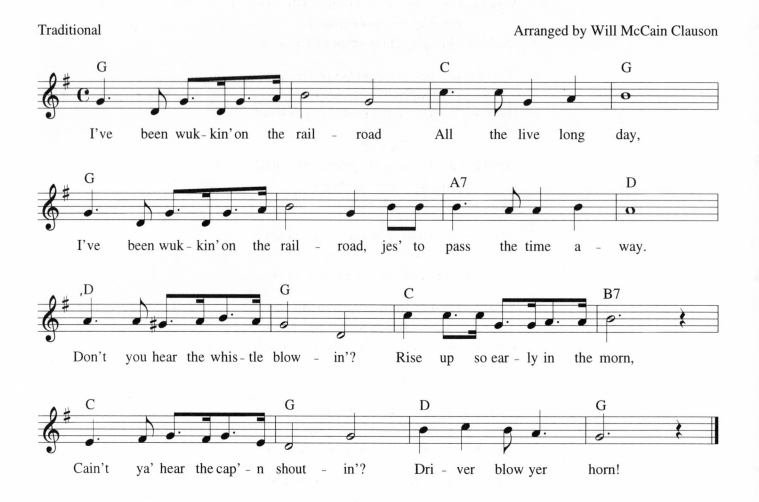

I'VE BEEN WUKKIN' ON THE RAILROAD

I've been wukkin' on the railroad,
All the live long day.
I've been wukkin' on the railroad,
Jes' to pass the time away.
Don'cha hear the whistle blowin'?
Rise up so early in the morn'.
Cain't ya hear the cap'n shoutin'?
Driver, blow yer horn.

I been wukkin' on the'railroad,
Spikin' rails all day,
I been wukkin' on the railroad,
I dun'no if I will stay.
Don'cha hear the shift boss callin',
Drive them spikes into the ties.
Cain'cha hear them sledges maulin',
And how the time jes' flies.

(cont. next page)

(cont.)

I been wukkin' with mah shovel,
Mah crow bar, and mah spade.
Jobbin' out here on the prairie,
Out along the railroad grade.
When we've dug on through to payday,
Our money's quickly sunk,
On the ladies, rum and whiskey,
Until we're all dead drunk!

(Repeat first verse.)

Express riders began to criss-cross the continent, while men were building a faster message carrier, the Overland Telegraph. The Indians found a new amusement in listening to the level "hum" of the "singing wires." Far less amusing to the native Americans was the coming of the steel roadway of the "beast" which they called "The Iron Horse."

The Iron Horse

(A Historical Letter Regarding Railroads)

President Andrew Jackson
Washington, D.C.

Dear Mr. President,

The canal system of this country is being threatened by the spread of a new form of transportation known as "Railroads." The Federal Government must preserve the canals for the following reasons:

One - if canal boats are supplanted by railroads, serious unemployment will result; captains, cooks, drivers, hostlers, repairmen and lock tenders will be left without means of livelihood, not to mention the numerous farmers now employed in growing hay for horses.

Two - boat builders are absolutely essential to the defense of the United States. In event of the expected trouble with England, the Erie Canal would be the only means by which we could ever move the supplies so vital to waging a modern war.

For the above mentioned reasons, the government should create an interstate commerce commission to protect the American people from the evils of railroads and to preserve the canals for prosterity.

As you may well know, Mr. President, 'railroad' carriages are pulled at the enormous speed of 15 miles per hour by engines which, in addition to endangering life and limb of passengers, roar and snort their way through the country-side, setting fire to crops, scaring the livestock and frightening women and children. The Almighty certainly never intended that people should travel at such breakneck speed.

Respectfully yours,

Martin Van Buren
Governor of New York

55

One of the greatest achievements of 19th century America was the arrival of the railroad. It was a new means of strengthening national unity, and for expansion. Our Country's 2,800 miles of track in 1840 were increased to 9,000 by 1850 and to 31,000 by 1860. The railroad giants raced to lay the most rail line, with the government giving vast parcels of land for every mile of track laid.

The Irish did the job for the Union Pacific, and thousands of Chinese, Mexican and Black laborers swung the picks and shovels to lay the tracks for the Central Pacific. The greatest triumph of railroading history came on May 10, 1869, when tracks of the Union Pacific met those of the Central Pacific at Promintory, Utah, with their tracks that ran 689 miles Eastward and 1,086 miles Westward.

To celebrate this historical moment, a golden spike was driven signifying the joining of the East and West. Americans now realized the much needed link between the West and the rest of the Nation, they were were no longer divided, and with that came all the color, and character, of what has come to be known as "The Wild West."

Cities sprang up around the railheads. Cattle were driven hundreds of miles to be freighted to the markets in the East. Immigrant settlers, pilgrims, and buffalo hunters rode the trains West. As a result, the face of "The Great American West" was greatly transformed. The train allowed many to venture West to search out and seize the bountiful treasure that awaited them.

It was 1831 when Americans got their first real train ride. It was on a small locomotive named "The Best Friend of Charleston." The tiny engine rattled and whizzed over six miles of track in South Carolina, pulling a flat car, (on which a cannon was mounted) followed by open carriages filled with exuberant men, women and children with the greatest of expectations. The passengers loved every jerk and jolt of the trip, as men in their tall stove-pipe hats fanned away for this special trip, and there were joyful salutes all along the way.

It reached the "amazing" speed of twenty-one miles per hour...totally unbelievable! In those days, a fifteen mile journey took at least two days. Roads were few, and they were terrible. Passengers in the crowded stagecoaches got so bounced and bruised that they preferred traveling on horse-back, whenever possible.

The Irishmen had this song to sing about layin' track, swingin' hammers, drillin' an' blasting rock, they were called the "tarriers."

> Drill ye tarriers, drill,
> Drill ye tarriers, drill!
> Oh, it's work all day,
> No sugar in yer tay!
> Workin' on the railway.
> **-Edited W M C**

They might not have sugar for their tea, but they did have their fill of buffalo meat, thanks to a "young man" by the name of Bill Cody. In the course of a year, Cody killed 4,280 of the beasts, and earned himself the title of "Buffalo Bill." The Railroaders thankfully made up a song about him:

> Buffalo Bill, Buffalo Bill,
> Always aims an' shoots to kill,
> Ain't never missed an' never will,
> The company pays his Buffalo Bill!
> **-Edited W M C**

JUST A COWHAND

Words & Music by
Will McCain Clauson

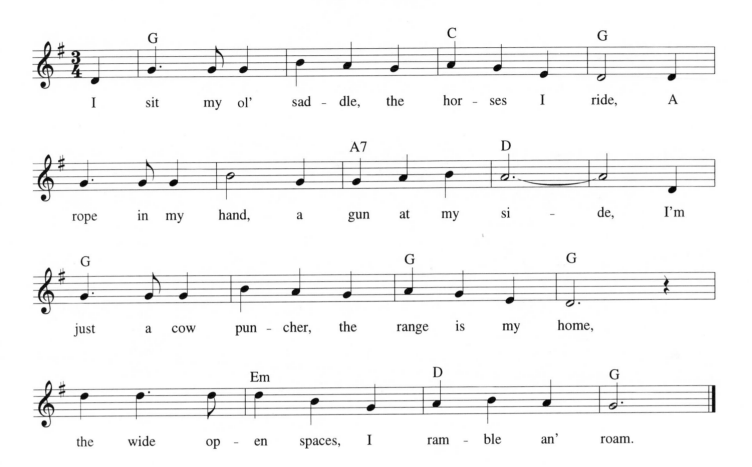

I sit my ol' sad-dle, the hor-ses I ride, A rope in my hand, a gun at my si - de, I'm just a cow pun - cher, the range is my home, the wide op - en spaces, I ram - ble an' roam.

JUST A COWHAND

I sit my old saddle, the horses I ride,
A rope in my hand, my gun at my side,
I'm just a cow puncher, the range is my home,
The wide open spaces, I ramble and roam.

Chorus:
Come a ki yi yippee yay-o, I'm just a cowhand,
A - rovin' and a - ropin' all over this land.

The sky is my ceiling, my bed the tall grass,
My lullaby's lowin' of herds as they pass.
The sun is my pardner, the pale moon my guide,
The stars light the trail, on the prairie I ride.

Chorus

The clouds are my pillow, I sleep and I dream,
And ponder my place in the Great Rancher's scheme.
My diggin's are furnished by the Almighty's hand,
He blessed me and keeps me, and gave me this land.

Chorus

LUCINDA

Words and Music by
Will McCain Clauson

Let me hold you in my lov- in' arms, Lu- cin- da, _____ An' I'll

prove to you my love's for- ev- er true. _____ May the

road I trav- el take me home, Lu- cin- da, _____ An' my

rov- in' eyes won't rove a- way from you. _____ Till the

riv- ers all run dry, you're my Lu- cin- da, _____ Till the

stars fall from the sky, I'll be your man. _____ Till my

dy- in' day you know I'll al- ways love you, _____ Please for-

give me, sweet Lu- cin- da, if you can. _____

LUCINDA

Let me hold you in my lovin' arms, Lucinda,
An' I'll prove to you my love's forever true.
May the road I travel lead me home, Lucinda,
An' my rovin' eyes won't rove away from you.

Till the rivers all run dry, you're my Lucinda,
Till the stars fall from the sky, I'll be your man.
· Till my dyin' day you know I'll always love you.
Please forgive me, sweet Lucinda, if you can.

Oh, your dark eyes shine like diamonds bright, Lucinda,
An' our nights of love mean more than I can say.
Dry those eyes and take me back just once again, girl.
Please don't let our dreams just die and fade away.

Oh, I know I let you down, my sweet Lucinda,
Life without you is so lonesome, I could cry.
I can't live without your lovin' arms around me,
Take me back to give our love another try.

PESSIMIST

It is easy to be grouchy,
When things ain't goin' yer way,
But the prize Ol' Growl,
Is the man who will howl,
When everything's goin' O.K.
-Anon.

THE WAY TO SUCCEED

"Push," sez the BUTTON.
"Take Pains," said the WINDOW.
"Never be led," warns the PENCIL.
"Be up to date," sez the CALENDAR.
"Make Light of Everything," sez the FIRE.
"Be sharp in your dealin's," sez the KNIFE.
"When ya' find a good thing, stick to it," said the GLUE.
- Anonymous

MAH SWISS MISS

New Words and Music Arranged
Will McCain Clauson

Oh, Ah, miss, mah Swiss miss, An' Mah

Swiss mis - ses me. She works

hard, in her yard, on her

knees, pun - chin' holes in my Swiss cheese. Oh, she

prom - ised to meet me, When the clock struck sev - en - teen, At the

stock - yard, Jes' fahve miles out - ta town Where the

hog's eyes, an' pig's ears, An' tuff ol' Tex - as steers, Sell for

sur - loin at nahn - teen cents a pound. _____

MAH SWISS MISS
(She Promised To Meet Me)

Oh, Ah miss, mah Swiss miss,
And mah Swiss misses me.
She works hard, in her yard, on her knees,
Punchin' holes in mah Swiss cheese.

Oh, she promised to meet me,
When the clock struck seventeen.
At the stockyard,
Jes' fahve miles outta town.
Where the hog's eyes, and pig's ears,
And tuff ol' Texas steers,
Sell for surloin at nahnteen cents a pound.

Oh, mah Swiss Miss, Ah miss her,
Ah miss the chance to kiss her,
She's pot-bellied, pig-tailed, but Ah'm her pal!
Oh, Ah know her teeth'r phoney,
From chawin' Swiss baloney
But Ah luv 'er, she's mah baby, she's mah gal!

Oh, Ah miss, mah Swiss miss,
And mah Swiss misses me.
She works hard, in her yard, on her knees,
Punchin' holes in mah Swiss cheese.

Oh, mah pickle face is humpy,
Her load is kinda lumpy.
She's cross-eyed, bow-legg'd, and pigeon-toed.
She's got ears like collie flowers,
And legs like Eiffel towers.
And her mug looks like two miles of bad road.

Oh, mah Swiss Miss, Ah miss her,
Ah miss the chance to kiss her,
She's knock-kneed, flat-footed, she's mah gal!
Oh, they say her breath is sweet,
But Ah'd ruther smell'r feet,
And ah miss, mah Swiss Miss, 'cuzz she's mah pal!

Oh, Ah miss, mah Swiss miss,
And mah Swiss misses me.
She works hard, in her yard, on her knees,
Punchin' holes in mah Swiss cheese.
Oh, she promised to meet me,
When the clock struck seventeen,
At the stockyard,
Jes' fahve miles outta town.
Where the hog's eyes, and pig's ears,
And tuff ol' Texas steers,
Sell for surloin at nahnteen cents a pound.

She's mah darlin', mah daisy,
She dang near drives me crazy,
She gives me bluegrass lovin', she's mah gal!
Her hair is red and frizzy,
Her block is sorta dizzy,
Halitosis, in her kisser, she's mah pal!

She's pure bliss, mah Swiss Miss,
And Ah miss that Swiss Miss kiss.
On mah knees, Ah beg ya' please, cum on back,
To punch holes in mah Swiss cheese.

61

MY LITTLE BROWN MULE

Words by N. Howard "Jack" Thorpe

Texas Tune Arranged and Adapted by
Will McCain Clauson

His Mam - my's a bur - ro, His Dad - dy's a

hoss. An' you might be a - think - in' It's a

might - y queer cross. Got brains in his

eyes, An' he ain't no fool,

Smart as a crick - et ____ , My lit - tle brown mule.

The words of "My Little Brown Mule" are by Nathan Howard "Jack" Thorpe. I have made only slight variations in his text, to accommodate the old Texas melody. Thorpe published and copyrighted the first collection of cowboy songs in 1908. The folk song scholars owe Thorpe a debt of gratitude for leading the way, for what is still "the cowboy singer's Bible" he was himself a great cowboy poet. It was in 1898 that he wrote the words to his most famous song, "Little Joe the Wrangler."

MY LITTLE BROWN MULE

His mammy's a burro,
His daddy's a hoss.
You might be a thinkin'
It's a mighty queer cross.
Got brains in his eyes,
An' he ain't no fool,
As smart as a cricket,
My little brown mule.

He's always in mischief,
He'll shy at a bug.
When he sees a Tin Lizzy
He'll jump like a frog.
A voice like a trumpet,
His coat's always bright.
He's gentle as can be,
If the cinch ain't too tight.

Jes' pull on that flank cinch
A little too long,
An' he won't do a thing
Til yer mounted and on.
Then farewell, relations,
Good-bye to the crowds.
Yer off on a journey
High up in the clouds.

At night I don't stake him,
Jes turn him foot loose.
Inside of two hours,
He's full as a goose.
A great ol' camp robber,
When the boys are in bed,
He'll root the chuck wagon
For bacon and bread.

He's a great one to wrangle,
He knows every hoss.
If one of 'em's missin',
He's mad as the boss.
His sense jes' comes natural,
He ain't been to school.
He's wise as a parson,
My little brown mule.

I ain't gonna sell him,
No, not on yer life.
The day we got hitched,
I gave him to the wife.
Now two of my kids
Ride him daily to school.
No money kin buy him,
My little brown mule.

MY LITTLE MOHEE

Traditional Words and Music
Edited by Will McCain Clauson

Arranged and Adapted by
Will McCain Clauson

As I was a wal - kin' _____ on a fine sum - mer day, I felt kin - da lone - some _____ as the hours flew a - way. So I sat down a dream - in' _____ a - lone on the grass, When who should stroll by me _____ but a young In - dian lass.

It was not unusual for the early mountaineers to adopt the Indian way of life and customs. Even their way of dress was Indian inspired. To this day, the Indians still make some of the mountain man clothing and beadwork seen at rendezvous. It was the Indian who showed the mountaineer how to survive in the vast wilderness. Mountain men and Indians, for the most part, were on friendly terms. Mixed marriages and courtships were common.

MY LITTLE MOHEE

As I was a walkin' on a fine summer day,
I felt kinda lonesome as the hours flew away.
So I sat down a dreamin' alone on the grass,
When who should stroll by me but a young Indian lass.

She sat down beside me, took hold of my hand,
She said, "You're a stranger from a faraway land,
But if you will follow, and come now with me,
I'll teach you the language of the little Mohee".

"Oh, no, dusky maiden, that never can be,
For I have a true love who is waitin' for me,
And I'll not forsake her, I know she loves me,
Her heart is as faithful as any could be.''

And so I sailed homeward to my own native land,
To my friends and relations, every welcomin' hand,
But of all those around me, not one did I see,
As eager to please me as my little Mohee.

The girl I had courted found another than me,
I left my own homeland, sailed 'cross the blue sea,
My course it was westward, away I did flee,
To dream all my daydreams with my little Mohee.

TAKE TIME

Take time to WORK,
It is the price of SUCCESS.
Take time to THINK,
It is the source of POWER.
Take time to PLAY,
It is the secret of YOUTH.
Take time to READ,
It is the foundation of WISDOM.
Take time to be FRIENDLY,
It is the road to HAPPINESS.
Take time to LOVE, and be LOVED,
It is pleasing to the LORD.
Take time to SHARE,
Life is too short to be selfish.
Take time to LAUGH,
LAUGHTER is the MUSIC OF THE SOUL.
- Author Unknown

NO, NO NEVER, NEVER, NO MORE

Trad. Irish/ Australian Melody
Arranged by Will Clauson

Original Words by Will McCain Clauson
and Howard "Chip" Culver

My back is sure ach - in', My seat's aw - ful sore, I'm

sick of cow - pun - chin', Cain't hack it no more. I'm

through eat - in' trail dust, I've had it with cows, I'm

tired of sheep - herd - ers, And Hay - seeds with plows. Oh, it's

no, no nev - er, _____ nev - er, no more, No, I

ain't gon - na be no cow - pun - cher no more.

NO, NO NEVER, NEVER, NO MORE

My back is sure achin',
My seat's awful sore,
I'm sick of cow punchin',
Cain't hack it no more.

I'm through eatin' trail dust,
I've had it with cows.
I'm tired of Sheepherder's
And Hayseeds with plows.

Chorus
Oh, it's no, no never, never, no more.
No, I ain't gonna be no cowpuncher no more!

They've plowed up the grassland,
They've fenced up the range.
I'm leavin' mañana,
I'm needin' a change.

I've been chousin' cattle,
For too many years,
I'm tired of lookin' up
Backsides of steers.

Chorus

I'm sellin' my saddle,
My chaps and my gear.
Good bye to the cayuse,
Good bye to the steer.

I'm off to the bright lights,
To drink up some cheer,
I'll be long gone tomorrow,
Don't look for me here.

Chorus

(Additional verse)
The life I was leadin',
Belongs in the past.
The West that I know, boys,
It ain't gonna last.

Hayseeds - Farmers   *Chousin' - Chasing*

OL' JOE CLARK

Arranged by Scott Reid
New & Old Words by Will McCain Clauson

Old Joe Clark's a mean ol' man, Mean as he kin be.

Knocked me down with his right hand, An' walked all ov - er me.

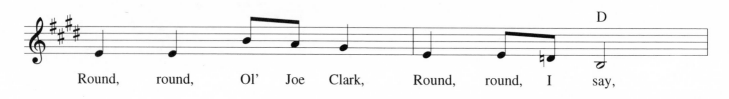

Round, round, Ol' Joe Clark, Round, round, I say,

Round, Round, Ol' Joe Clark, I ain't got long to stay.

OL' JOE CLARK

Square Dance Tune
Arr. Scott Reid

New & Trad. Words
Will McCain Clauson

Ol' Joe Clark's a mean ol' man,
Mean as he kin be.
Knocked me down with his right hand,
And walked all over me.

Chorus:
Round, round, Ol' Joe Clark,
Round, round, I say.
Round, round, Ol' Joe Clark,
I ain't got long to stay.

He drinks the rye and shoots the breeze,
Ya' ought to hear him brag.
He never offers me no drink,
That low down scalawag.

(cont. next page)

Chorus repeats

If ya' see that scalawag,
Tell him if ya' can,
Before he goes to make the mash,
To wash them dirty hands.

Chorus repeats

Ol' Joe Clark, he's gotta a hound,
Blind as he can be.
Chases 'possums 'round an' 'round,
And 'coons up a holler tree.

Chorus repeats

When Ol' Joe comes to my door,
He treats me like a pup.
Runs my bear dawg under the floor,
An' drinks mah whiskey up.

Chorus repeats

Ya' kin ride my ol' gray mare,
Ya' kin ride my Roan,
Ya' kin pick on my git-tar,
But leave my gal alone!

Chorus repeats

If I had a rawhide rope,
I'd make a loop 'n' throw,
Throw it 'round some purdy gal,
An' down the road we'd go.

Chorus repeats

If I had a candy box,
To put my sweetheart in,
I'd take her out 'n' kiss her twice,
An' put her back again.

Chorus repeats

Ol' Joe Clark, he's gone away,
Gone, I don't know whar,
Some goes up and some goes down,
He's gone away down thar.

Chorus repeats

He puts his banjo in mah hand,
Tells me what to play,
Dances with mah own true love,
Until the break of day.

Chorus repeats

Ol' Joe Clark he had a cow,
That crossed a freezin' stream,
Dragged her udders on the ice.
An' now she gives ice cream.

Additional chorus:
Git out the way, Ol' Joe Clark,
Hide that jug a wine.
Git out the way, Ol' Joe Clark,
Yer no friend of mine.

PAT MALONE FORGOT THAT HE WAS DEAD

Source: Waldo "Swede" Larson

Melody Arr. and Adapt.
by Will McCain Clauson

Times were hard in I - rish town, Ev' - ry - thing was go - ing down, ___ And
wife spoke up and said, "Now, dear Pat, if you were dead, ___ That

Pat Ma - lone was pushed for rea - dy cash. ___ He for
twen - ty thou - sand dol - lars we could take." ___ And so

life in - sur - ance spent, All his mo - ney to a cent, ___ So
Pat laid down and tried, to make out that he had died, ___ Un -

all of his af - fairs had gone ker - smash! ___ But his Then
til he smelt the whis - key at the wake. ___

Chorus

Pat Ma - lone for - got that he was dead. ___ He raised him - self and

shout - ed from the bed, ___ "If this wake goes on a min - ute The

corpse he must be in it, You'll have to get me drunk to keep me dead." ___ Then they

Waldo Larson sang his version of this whimsical ballad. I had seen it earlier in print with an entirely different melody. I suspect that Waldo unknowingly wrote his own melody. He said, "I don't rightly know; it's been so long ago." Waldo began cowboying at the age of 14. He related to me the fact that "many a cowboy simply put their own melodies to words they happened to run across'.' Since many of the early day cowboys were of Irish extraction, this one from the old sod was rowdily sung and passed on in the folk tradition.

70

PAT MALONE FORGOT THAT HE WAS DEAD

Times were hard in Irish town,
Ev'ry thing was going down,
And Pat Malone was pushed for ready cash.
He for life insurance spent,
All his money to a cent,
An' all of his affairs had gone ker-smash.

But his wife spoke up and said,
"Now, dear Pat, if you were dead,
That twenty thousand dollars we could take."
And so Pat lay down and tried,
To make out that he had died,
Until he smelt the whiskey at the wake!

Chorus
Then Pat Malone forgot that he was dead.
He raised himself and shouted from the bed.
"If this wake goes on a minute,
The corpse he must be in it,
You'll have to get me drunk to keep me dead!"

Then they gave the corpse a sup,
Afterwards they filled him up,
And laid him out again upon the bed.
Then before the mornin' gray,
All their cares had passed away,
They all forgot he only played off dead!

So they took him from the bunk,
Still alive, but awful drunk,
And put him in a coffin with a pray'r.
But the driver of the cart,
Said "Be-dad, I'll never start,
Until I see that someone pays the fare!"

Chorus
Then Pat Malone forgot that he was dead.
He sat up in the coffin while he said,
"If you dare to doubt my credit,
You'll be sorry that you said it.
Drive on or else the corpse'll break your head!"

So the funeral started out,
On the cemetery route,
And the neighbors tried the widow to console,
Till they stopped beside the base,
Of Malone's last resting place,
And gently lowered Patrick in the hole.

Then Malone began to see,
Just as plain as one, two, three,
That he'd forgot to reckon on the end!
So, as clods began to drop,
He broke off the coffin top,
And to the earth he quickly did ascend!

Chorus
Then Pat Malone forgot that he was dead.
And from the cemetery quickly fled!
He came nearly going under,
It's a lucky thing by thunder,
That Pat Malone forgot that he was dead!

POLLY WOLLY DOODLE

New Verses by Howard "Chip" Culver
and Will McCain Clauson

Trad. American Folk Arrangement
Will McCain Clauson

Oh, I had a horse, and his name was Jack, Sing Pol – ly, wol – ly, doo – dle all the day. I put him in the barn, And he jumped through a crack, Sing Pol – ly, wol – ly, doo – dle all the day. Fare thee well, Fare thee well, Fare thee well, my mer – ry Fay. Oh, I'm goin' to Lou' – si – an – a, For to see my Sus – ie An – na. Sing, Pol – ly, wol – ly, doo – dle all the day.

POLLY WOLLY DOODLE

Oh, I had a horse,
And his name was Jack.
Sing Polly, wolly, doodle all the day.
I put him in the barn,
And he jumped through a crack.
Sing Polly, wolly, doodle all the day.

(cont.)

Chorus:
Fare thee well,
Fare the well,
Fare the well, my merry Fay.
Oh, I'm goin' to Lou'siana,
For to see my Susie Anna.
Sing Polly, wolly, doodle all the day.

Oh, I had a dog,
And his name was Rover,
Sing Polly, wolly, doodle all the day.
When the poor thing died,
He died all over.
Sing Polly, wolly, doodle all the day.

Chorus

Oh, I had a pig,
And his name was Stash.
Sing Polly, wolly, doodle all the day.
He loved to git smashed,
On whiskey mash.
Sing Polly, wolly, doodle all the day.

Chorus

Oh, I had a duck,
And his name was Quack,
Sing Polly, wolly, doodle all the day.
He went down to the river,
And never came back.
Sing Polly, wolly, doodle all the day.

Chorus

Oh, my rooster got
The pippin'-cough,
Sing Polly, wolly, doodle all the day
He coughed his comb,
And tail right off,
Sing Polly, wolly, doodle all the day.

Chorus

I had a hen,
And she had a wooden leg.
Sing Polly, wolly, doodle all the day.
She'd hop to the coop,
And lay a wooden egg.
Sing Polly, wolly, doodle all the day.

Chorus

Oh, I had a cow,
And her name was Silk.
Sing Polly, wolly, doodle all the day.
When I pulled her udder,
She squirted buttermilk.
Sing Polly, wolly, doodle all the day.

Chorus

Oh, there's bread and cheese,
Upon the shelf.
Sing Polly, wolly, doodle all the day.
If you want any more,
Go, sing it yourself
Sing Polly, wolly, doodle all the day.

Chorus

PRESS ALONG TO THE BIG CORRAL

Cowboy Song Arr. & Adapt.
Will McCain Clauson

That bo - vine brute from the cat - tle chute, Press a -
long to the big cor - ral, He should be bran - ded
on the snoot, Press a - long to the big cor - ral.

Chorus:

Press a - long, Cow - boy, Press a - long with a Cow - boy
yell. Press a - long, with a
great big nose, press a - long to the big cor - ral!

Cowboys would never sing a ballad like this within audible distance of the camp cook, whom their very lives depended upon as some of the trail drives took from two - three months. All the hands would show him the greatest respect while in camp. When he wasn't around they would refer to him as "the old woman," "Cookie," etc.

PRESS ALONG TO THE BIG CORRAL

That bovine brute from the cattle chute,
Press along to the big corral,
He should be branded on the snoot,
Press along to the big corral.

Chorus:
Press along, Cowboy,
Press along, with a Cowboy yell,
Press along, with a great big noise,
Press along to the big corral!

(Repeat same pattern as above for following verses using these couplets:)

It's every day 'bout half past four,
He opens up his mouth to roar.

It's "Wake up, boys" he starts to shout,
We hit the grit to tough it out.

It's boiled sowbelly ev'ry day,
An' always fixed the same ol' way.

He always gives us more'n enough,
Of S.O.S.—the "Same Ol' Stuff!"

Sidepork and beans out on the range,
We ain't about to git no change!

MULES
(To the tune of Auld Lang Syne)

On mules we find, two legs behind,
And two we find before.
We stand behind, before we find,
What the two behind be for.

When we're behind, the two behind,
We find what they be for.
So, stand before, the two behind,
Behind the two before.
- Anonymous

RED RIVER VALLEY

Traditional Melody, Arr. by
Will McCain Clauson

New Words by
Anthony Wayne Webner III

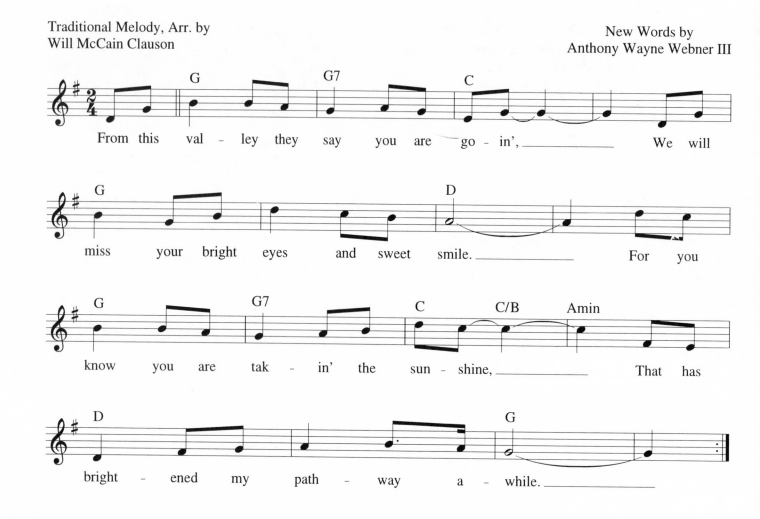

From this val - ley they say you are go - in', _____ We will
miss your bright eyes and sweet smile. _____ For you
know you are tak - in' the sun - shine, _____ That has
bright - ened my path - way a - while. _____

RED RIVER VALLEY

From this valley they say you are goin',
We will miss your bright eyes and sweet smile,
For you know that you're takin' the sunshine,
That has brightened my pathway a while.

Come and sit by my side if you love me,
Do not hasten to bid me adieu,
But remember the Red River Valley,
And the cowboy who loves you so true.

Oh, the winds of the prairies blow lonely,
Cold and restless, I wander alone,
But the light from your love that I carry,
Will warm me wherever I roam.

West, I ride, to the land of Eldorado.
East, you're bound, to the bright lights aglow.
Though apart, we will meet once again, dear,
In the vale where we loved long ago.

Down a river of dreams we'll drift homeward,
And though far, we may ramble and roam,
We'll remember our valley of love, dear,
And follow the Red River home.

Come and sit by my side, little darlin',
Do not hasten to bid me adieu,
But remember the Red River valley,
And the cowboy who loves you so true.

Make sure yer on the right TRAIL before ya' RIDE.

-W M C

Travis "Nick" Merritt

My friend, Nick, spoke with a kind of Midwestern accent even though he was born, lived, and worked in Texas. "They tell me I was born in Van Horn Texas, but I don't remember the event," he said jokingly. "Maybe some of the real old timer's talked with what you think of as a Western accent, but we called our hosses 'horses'," he answered, in response to my noting that his "drawl" was missing.

After that was settled, he continued, "When I was about eleven years old, I started working with W.T. Wimberly, my neighbor, doin' whatever work he had for me do, from gatherin' up cows for brandin', mendin' fences, etc."

"My father had what was considered a small ranch back then, about 50,000 acres, and 100 head of cattle or so. He gave me the job of takin' care of them when I was about thirteen. He only had some five sections that he owned, a section being 640-720 acres in those parts. Later on he bought two more sections. The ranch was fifty miles north of Van Horn, and about 20 miles from the New Mexico state line.

"My neighbor, 'W.T.,' moved about seventy miles from there when I was 17, I went along to help move his cattle. When I was workin' cattle, what the 'old timers' called open range was mostly gone. Several ranchers would get together and use the same ground to run their cattle. Open range pretty much ran out when the barb wire fences started comin'.

"I did whatever it took to stay alive, work wise, I built a lot of fences. In fact, one winter during the depression, Dad, my brother, me, and another boy, built over twenty-five miles of fence.

"As I got older, I worked for other outfits in the area. A big one came in from South Texas, on a ranch about five miles east of us. I'd work bringin' in cattle from the range, or drivin' 'em to them.

"We'd take 300-500 head sometimes. The approximate 70 miles would take us a good ten days, and then three days to bring the horses back to the ranch after we left the critters. Of course, only one or two of us would be left to mind the horses. The other cowboys went their own way, at the end of the drive, goin' back to their families, or some other drive.

"In 1937, I went to work for The Palomas Land & Cattle Company. They had a large ranch in Old Mexico, and another on this side of the border. I worked for them for about four years. They had 714 sections that they either leased or owned. The ranch started 18 miles East of El Paso and ran to the eighty-mile marker on the highway, between El Paso and Carlsbad.

"That's where I got into the big cattle drives, and we did have some big ones. Mexicans would gather the cattle in Mexico and bring 'em over to the stockyards in El Paso, up to the railway.

"We'd go into El Paso from the ranch, and pick up these cattle when they'd come in. Sometimes the herds were small, only 700-800 head, but at times we'd get as many as 5000. We'd get two or three different bunches a year, and take 'em out to the range in the fall. They wintered there, then in the early spring we'd round 'em up, and take 'em back to El Paso. They were then shipped out to Kansas, or wherever they might be headed.

"One trip, when we were gettin' about 5000 cows from Old Mexico, they also sent us about 28 head of horses. We knew they were comin' so we didn't take back up mounts. These horses were gentle alright, the Mexicans had just about worn 'em out by the time we got 'em. A hard-lookin' bunch they were!

"We took 'em out there to the ranch that fall when we got through workin' with 'em and turned 'em out on the range. We didn't do anythin' with 'em until spring came, and I'll tell you, when we gathered 'em up again, they weren't near as gentle! Pretty lively and rank they were!

"When I'd been there a few years, they gave me the job of distributin' the cows to the larger waterin' holes. After we took 'em out to the range, I'd stay an' get 'em all settled while the rest of the hands went back for another herd.

"We only had Anglos workin' on the ranch, because the Mexicans couldn't come across the Rio Grande River. We met 'em at the bridge to collect the cows. Sometimes it was a river, sometimes it was just a 'trickle.' Other times you could step acrost it an' never wet yer feet. When it was really big we called it Ol' Muddy."

When I asked him about entertainment, he replied, "We didn't have much time for that. We did have one guy, who worked with us, who had a 2-door '30's' Ford, with the whole back seat full of musical instruments. I mean, he had everythin'! Banjo, fiddle, squeeze box, harmonica...and he could play the works...anythin' he could pick up! He'd give us more entertainment than we needed after work.

"The steady hands on all the bigger spreads stayed in bunkhouses. There wasn't a lot to do when we weren't working. Sometimes we played cards, but not a great lot, and did a little readin'. We didn't tell stories much. I guess there weren't too many stories that hadn't already been heard.

"Folks would have barn dances around the country-side. Sometimes we'd drive over fifty miles for a good party. We'd get together maybe once or twice a month, less often when the weather was bad. I always had a good time, even when I didn't have a date. A few of the boys drank, but most of us didn't.

"We'd take time to go to Flagstaff or Williams, Arizona. They had rodeos every Sunday, an' all of us would go to 'em an' participate. I team-tied some, and did some calf-ropin'. The Indians had a rodeo too, and a big pow-wow up there that I liked to go to.

"There wasn't much in the way of church goin' in those parts. Most of the ranches were too far out,

some up to fifty miles. We'd only go into town about once a month, dependin' on what was needed. Sometimes we wouldn't get to town for two or three months!

"Always had good food on the trail. A full crew was 16-22 men. At The Palomas we butchered a beef once a week just to feed 'em. We were lucky because the same Cook signed on almost every year." Nick's eyes lit up as he continued, "That man was an ARTIST with SOURDOUGH buns," he exclaimed, with his mouth watering. "Boy, were they good! He cooked 'em on coals in a three legged, cast-iron pot, called a Dutch Oven. So they'd bake evenly all over, he'd put coals on the lid too."

"I also can't forget them 'frijole' beans and beef, nearly every meal, along with whatever else he'd surprise us with. When we were out working, the chuckwagon went right along with us. We'd tell the cook every morning where to meet us for lunch, or dinner."

I asked Nick if the cowboys ever said "grace". He seemed puzzled, but then did remember one:

"Bless the meat,
Dang the skin,
Back yer ears,
Let's DIVE IN!"
Amen

"The wrangler moved the horses with the chuckwagon, and helped the cook out, got wood for him and such. We seldom had chili, but lots of stews and fried meat and gravy, he was a good cook—really put out the food. 'Pertaters,' canned stuff like 'Termaters.' We had dried fruit (apples or apricots). Not too many greens to be had."

I asked him, "Did ya' carry guns?" "No," he replied, "maybe a rifle for huntin'. I had a pistol in my bedroll, but I never carried it because there was no need for it."

"When I got married, a friend of mine talked me into taking care of a spread he had in Woodside,

Ya' cain't make BREAD if ya' ain't got the DOUGH.

-W M C

78

Utah, on the Price River, which was full of alkali. I bought a bunch of calves and fed 'em through the winter on corn silage left over from the harvest. We had a small garden, I don't know how it grew with all that alkali, but it did good. After that, we went back to Ash Fork, where I went to work on another ranch, and then on to Prescott and Payson, Arizona, where I did 'weekend' ranchin' an' cowboyin'."

"Why did you quit cowboyin'?" I asked. "The money just wasn't there. You could make more doin' almost anything else. I got a dollar a day when I was a kid, plus a meal. The Palomas paid GOOD, $45.00/month with lots of room and board! Doing 'day work' at the time was just $2.00 a day. Back in the old days, mostly it was a mere $30.00 a month. The cook got more, and the wrangler usually got less, though he worked harder than most of the hands.

"I reckon I spent practically all my life under a hat, except when I was sleepin'. My memory don't keep up with me as much as it used to, but I must have spent a good 35-40 years in the saddle."

I asked him, once again, how old he was, and he told me, with a chuckle, "Don't ask me that again, I CAN'T remember...had TOO many birthdays to recall when the FIRST one was!"

TO MY PARDNER

Source: Yardley   Edited: Clauson

When you ain't got a penny,
And yer feelin' kinda blue,
With a cloud a hangin' over
That won't let sunshine thro',
It's a pleasant sorta feelin',
For a pardner just to lay
A HAND UPON YER SHOULDER,
In a friendly sorta way.

It's kinda tough when yer a man,
And feel a tear drop start,
When ya' feel a kinda flutter,
In the region of yer heart.
Ya' cain't look up and meet his eye,
Ya' don't have words to say,
When a HAND IS ON YER SHOULDER,
In a friendly sorta way.

This world's a contradict'ry place,
With its honey and its gall,
Its cares, and bitter crosses,
But a good world after all.
And a good God musta made it,
That's all I've gotta say,
When a HAND IS ON YER SHOULDER,
In a friendly sorta way.

79

RIDIN' OL' PAINT

Traditional Words & Music
Arr. by Will McCain Clauson

Ri – din' Ol' Paint, lea – din' Ol' Dan.

Go – in' to Mon – tan'_____ to throw the hou – li – han. They

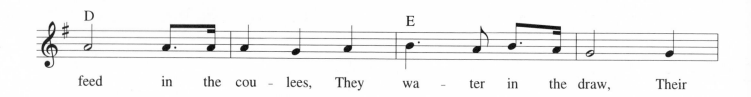

feed in the cou – lees, They wa – ter in the draw, Their

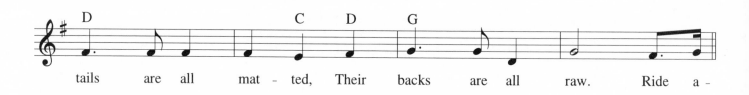

tails are all mat – ted, Their backs are all raw. Ride a –

roun', lit – tle do _____ gies, Ride a – roun' 'em slow, fer the

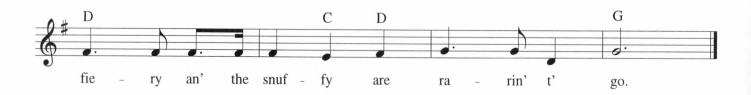

fie – ry an' the snuf – fy are ra – rin' t' go.

RIDIN' OL' PAINT

Ridin' Ol' Paint,
Leadin' Ol' Dan,
Goin' to Montan,
T' throw the houlihan.
They feed in the coulees,
They water in the draw,
Their tails are all matted,
Their backs are all raw.

Chorus:
Ride aroun', little dogies,
Ride aroun' 'em slow,
Fer the firey an' the snuffy,
Are rarin' t' go.

When I die,
Take my saddle from the wall,
Put it on my pony,
Lead 'im out of his stall.
Tie my bones to his back,
Turn our faces t'ward the West,
An' we'll ride the prairies,
That we love the best.

The Harvey Girls

A fairer maiden I shall never see,
She was winsome, she was neat,
She was gloriously sweet.
And she certainly was very good to me.
- Unknown

Frederick Henry Harvey left London in 1850 to seek his fortune in the New World. Eventually, he commanded a catering empire of forty-seven depot diners and restaurants; fifteen railroad hotels and thirty dining cars. For the first time in the West, a railroad became famous for its food.

One cowboy said, "They make ya' take off yer hat and put on a coat, but the grub is strictly 'A' Number One!" The cowboys were more than impressed with the beautiful waitresses that Harvey employed. He advertised for "young women of good character, attractive and intelligent."

They came in droves, making a salary of $17.50 a month, plus room and board, and tips. Harvey provided a dormitory with a chaperoned "courtin' parlor," but with, to the disappointment of the cowboys, a 10:00 p.m. curfew. The Harvey girls dazzled the lonely Westerners and helped populate the West by marrying approximately 5,000 of them.

Ya' ain't RICH if ya' only got MONEY.
-W.M.C

SALVAGE, RECYCLE
(Help Save a Song)

Words and Music by Will McCain Clauson

We did-n't have mo-tor cars, or big air - y planes, _____ 'n no tal - kin' pitch - ures, or stream - line - ded trains. But we had the fa - mi - ly, 'n' we had the songs. We'd sing - 'em to - ge - ther, 'n' pass 'em a - long. Pass 'em

Chorus

on, pass 'em on. Don't throw 'em _____ a - way. Use 'em, don't lose 'em, We want 'em to stay. Pass 'em on, Pass 'em on, as you go on your way. Sal - vage, Re - cy - cle, 'n' Sing some each day.

SALVAGE, RECYCLE
Help Save A Song

We didn't have motor cars,
Or big, airy - planes,
'n' no talkin' pitchers,
Or stream - line - ded trains.
But, we had the fa - mi - ly,
'n' we had the songs.
We'd sing 'em together.
'n' pass 'em along.

PASS 'EM ON, PASS 'EM ON,
Don't throw 'em away.
Use 'em, don't lose 'em,
We wan' 'em to stay.
PASS 'EM ON, PASS 'EM ON,
As you go on your way.
SALVAGE, RECYCLE,
'n' SING some each day.

Ma played the dul - ci - mer,
'n' Pa fiddled some.
Sandy played man - do - lin,
'n' Grandpa would hum.
We sang in the parlor,
Played musical games.
Them songs, they ain't sung now,
I think it's a shame.

PASS 'EM ON, PASS 'EM ON,
Don't throw 'em away.
Strum 'em, or hum 'em,
We wan' 'em to stay.
PASS 'EM ON, PASS 'EM ON,
Keep singin' a song.
SALVAGE, RECYCLE,
'n' HELP 'em live on.

My brothers and sisters,
Would learn all the songs.
They'd join in the chorus,
And all sing along.
Them good days are over,
The fam'ly is gone.
I sit here alone, now,
Jes' hummin' a song.

PASS 'EM ON, PASS 'EM ON,
As you go on your way.
Sing 'em. don't fling 'em,
Or toss 'em away.
PASS 'EM ON, PASS 'EM ON.
Keep singin' a song.
SALVAGE, RECYCLE,
'n' pass 'em along.

They could sound as good,
As they did once before,
If we'd git together,
'n' sing 'em some more.
If I had a choice, now,
I'd bring back them days,
Of long, long ago,
'n' the ol' fashion'd ways.

PASS 'EM ON, PASS 'EM ON,
Don't toss 'em away.
Use 'em, don't lose 'em,
They're welcome to stay.
SING A SONG, SING A SONG,
Make the world hum along.
SALVAGE, RECYCLE,
'n' help SAVE a song.

COWBOY BASICS

Somethin' ON 'im,
Somethin' IN 'im,
Wide open spaces,
AROUND 'im,
A good horse BENEATH 'im,
The big sky ABOVE 'im,
A gal BESIDE 'im...
TO LOVE 'IM.
- Will McCain Clauson

SEE YA' ON SUNDAY
(If the Weather's Good)

Words and music by
Will McCain Clauson

(to be sung one-octave lower)

Let's all git to-geth-er, if the crick don't rise, Let's

all git to-geth-er, it would be so nice, let's all git to-geth-er, let's

all git to-geth-er, let's all git to-geth-er, if the crick don't rise. Let's

Chorus

all git to-geth-er if the wea-ther's good, let's all git to-geth-er if the

wea-ther's good. Let's all git to-geth-er, let's all git to-geth-er, Let's

all git to-geth-er, if the wea-ther's good. We'll

SEE YA' ON SUNDAY

Let's all git together, if the crick don't rise,
Let's all git together, it would be so nice,
Let's all git together, let's all get together,
Let's all git together, if the crick don't rise.

Chorus:
Let's all git together if the weather's good,
Let's all git together if the weather's good.
Let's all git together, let's all git together,
Let's all git together if the weather's good.

We'll see ya' on Sunday, if the wind don't blow.
We'll see ya' on Sunday, if there ain't no snow,
We'll see ya' on Sunday, we'll see ya' on Sunday,
We'll see ya' on Sunday, if the wind don't blow.

Repeat Chorus

Y'all come an' join us, if the road is good,
Y'all come an' join us, 'cause ya' know ya' should,
Y'all come an' join us, y'all come and join us.
Y'all come an' join us, if the road is good.

Repeat Chorus

So hitch up the wagon, for a Sunday ride,
'Cause everybody's comin' from afar an' wide.
Go hitch up your wagon, an' don't ya' be draggin',
There's no time for laggin' on a Sunday ride.

Repeat Chorus

The Lord we'll be praisin', come and join the throng,
Our voices we'll be raisin' in a joyful song,
Let's all git together, in spite of the weather,
Go hitch up your wagon an' y'all come along.

Dont' STOP what you've BEGUN,
UNTIL it' all DONE.
✦✦✦✦✦✦
LOVE and FRIENDSHIP,
The best GIFTS ya' kin give.
✦✦✦✦✦✦
A GUILTY man RUNS from his own shadow.
The pangs of VICE,
Ain't worth the PRICE.
✦✦✦✦✦✦
The more a man GITS,
The more a man WANTS.

- W M C

SHEKELS OF SHAME

Words and music by
Will McCain Clauson

Thir - ty piec - es of sil - ver, _____ dir - ty shek - els of shame, _____ was the price paid for Je - sus, _____ on the cross He was slain. _____ Be - trayed and for - sa - ken _____ by one who would claim, _____ thir - ty pie - ces of sil - ver, _____ dir - ty shek - els of shame. Ju - das said to the

SHEKELS OF SHAME

Thirty pieces of silver,
Dirty shekels of shame,
Was the price paid for Jesus.
On the cross he was slain.
Betrayed and forsaken,
By one who would claim,
Thirty pieces of silver,
Dirty shekels of shame.

Judas said to the council,
That our Lord he'd betray.
Thirty pieces of silver,
Was the price they would pay.
Thirty pieces of silver,
And our Saviour was sold,
To the Pharisee council,
And the high priests of old.

Judas led them to Jesus,
And they found Him in prayer.
The kiss of betrayal,
Was our Saviour's despair.
They mocked and reviled Him,
And led Him away,
A man of great sorrow,
On a blood sprinkled way.

Then they crowned our dear Saviour
With thorns 'round his head,
And the rainment of purple
Showed the bloodstains red.
In remorse, and in sorrow,
With the heart full of strife,
Greed and envy had earned him,
Judas took his own life.

Thirty pieces of silver,
Dirty shekels of shame,
Was the price paid for Jesus.
Tho' he died not in vain.
Our Lord and Redeemer.
His life chose to give,
On a hillside in Calv'ry,
So that mankind might live.

DEATH: Bein' on the "no breakfast forever list."
-Source: Katie Lee

ABSENT from the body...PRESENT with the Lord.
-Source: The Good Book

SHE'LL BE COMIN' 'ROUND THE MOUNTAIN

Words and Music Arr. and Adapt. by
Will McCain Clauson

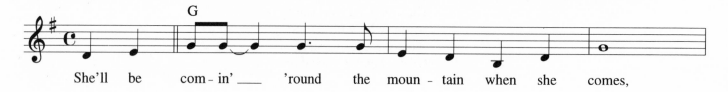

SHE'LL BE COMIN' 'ROUND THE MOUNTAIN

She'll be comin' 'round the mountain when she comes,
She'll be comin' 'round the mountain when she comes,
She'll be goin' like the devil,
On his way to lower level,
She'll be comin' 'round the mountain when she comes.

She'll be a huffin' an' a puffin' when she comes,
She'll be a huffin' an' a puffiin' when she comes,
She'll be a huffin' an' a puffin',
The conductor is a tough'n,
He will throw ya' off fer nothin', when she comes.

Oh, the brakeman and the stoker when she comes,
Oh, the brakeman and the stoker when she comes,
Oh, the brakeman and the stoker,
Will be playin' liar's poker,
An' the brakeman gits the joker when she comes.

We'll be eatin' chicken 'n' dumplin's when she comes,
We'll be eatin' chicken 'n' dumplin's when she comes,
Oh, it's always chicken weather,
When the rounders git together,
We'll be eatin' chicken 'n' dumplin's when she comes.

There will be a celebration when she comes,
There will be a celebration when she comes,
There will be a celebration,
When she rolls into the station,
There will be a celebration when she comes.

She'll be comin' 'round the mountain when she comes,
She'll be comin' 'round the mountain when she comes,
She'll be comin' 'round the mountain,
An' the crew will be a-shoutin',
She'll be comin' 'round the mountain when she comes.

Originally, the melody of the above tune was a spiritual, "The Old Ship Of Zion." These days the youngsters have their own special version, which has nothing to do with railroading. The pick and shovel men sang a version similar to the one given here, minus the unprintable verses.

THAT MAN IN THE GLASS

When ya' git what ya' want in yer struggle fer self,
An' the world makes ya' King fer a day,
Go to the mirror an' look at yerself,
An' see what THAT MAN'S got to say.

It ain't yer Mother, er Father, er Wife,
Whose judgment upon ya' must pass,
But the feller whose verdict should count in yer life,
Is the MAN lookin' back from the glass.

Ya' might fool the world, down the long trail of years,
An' get pats on yer back as ya' pass,
But yer final reward will be HEARTACHES an' TEARS,
If you've cheated THAT MAN IN THE GLASS.

If you kin please HIM, don't mind all the rest,
HE'S with ya' right to the END,
Be true to HIM. You've passed the test,
If THAT MAN lookin' back is yer FRIEND.
-Unknown Author
Source: Dave Sherwood - Edited by Will McCain Clauson

SLEEP, DOGIE, SLEEP

Words and music by
Will McCain Clauson

SLEEP, DOGIE, SLEEP

Out under starry skies,
Far from the ki-yotes cries,
I'll hum ya' lullabies.
SLEEP, DOGIE, SLEEP.

From cold winds you kin hide,
Warm by yer mother's side,
Out on the prairie wide.
SLEEP, DOGIE, SLEEP.

Wrapped in a moonlit beam,
Dreamin' of milk and cream,
Cool streams, and clover green.
SLEEP, DOGIE, SLEEP.

SUCCESS

The father of SUCCESS is WORK. The mother of SUCCESS is AMBITION. The oldest son is COMMON SENSE. Some of the other boys are: PERSEVERANCE, HONESTY, THOROUGHNESS, FORESIGHT, ENTHUSIASM and COOPERATION. The oldest daughter is CHARACTER. Some of her sisters are: CHEERFULNESS, LOYALTY, CARE, COURTESY, ECONOMY, SINCERITY, and HARMONY. The baby is OPPORTUNITY.

Get acquainted with the "OLD MAN" and you will be able to get along pretty well with the rest of the family.

-Anonymous

A BIG, TALL ONE

My pardner, Slim, wuz a great one fer exaggeratin'.

"She had a heart as BIG as the state of Texas," he said to me one day, "an' I LOVED every part o' her. But, she wuz SO BIG that to hug 'er all over would take me almost a week!"

"When I'd go a-courtin', I'd have to take along a piggin' string an' some chalk, to section 'er off. I wanted to make sure I didn't miss any part of 'er. It was HUGGIN' an' a CHALKIN', so ter speak, but well worth the effort."

"One week, when I'd finally worked my way around to the front, I wuz TOTALLY dumbfoozled at what I saw. ANOTHER Cowpoke...with a long piggin' string...an' a whole bucket o' chalk. That son of a so an' so had bin workin' his way around the OTHER side o' her spread!"

"I grabbed his bucket, hit 'im on the head, an' dusted 'im off, real good. I gave up on HUGGIN' fer a LONG TIME after that!"

- As related to Will McCain Clauson

THAT WAS THE LIFE OF THE COWBOY

Trad. Adapt. & Arr.
Will McCain Clauson

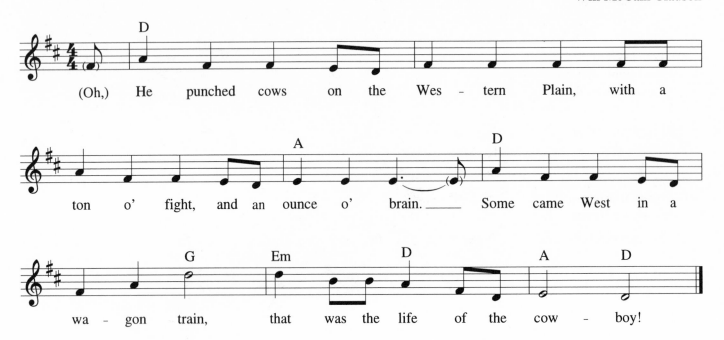

(Oh,) He punched cows on the Wes – tern Plain, with a ton o' fight, and an ounce o' brain. ____ Some came West in a wa – gon train, that was the life of the cow – boy!

THAT WAS THE LIFE OF THE COWBOY

He punched cows on the Western Plain,
With a ton o' fight and an ounce o' brain.
Some came West in a wagon train,
THAT WAS THE LIFE OF THE COWBOY.

He laughed at death and he scoffed at life,
He had t' go it without a wife.
He fought with pistol, rifle er knife,
THAT WAS THE LIFE OF THE COWBOY.

He'd set up drinks when he hadn't a cent,
He'd fight like hell with a tinhorn gent.
When he made love he'd go hell bent,
THAT WAS THE LIFE OF THE COWBOY.

He'd shoot out lights in a Dancin' Hall,
He'd git shot up in a drunken brawl.
Some cor'ners jury would end it all,
THAT WAS THE END OF THE COWBOY.

-Melody adapted from an old time cowboy dance, "I Wonder," new and traditional words by Will McCain Clauson.

Lloyd "Buckskin" Robinson

"My folks homesteaded in Colorado, just seven miles south of the Missouri Pacific, in Kansas," said Lloyd "Buckskin" Robinson. "Both of 'em filed on adjoining pieces since they each could git a quarter section, an' got a half section that way. I was born in Tribune, it was prairie country and almost everything was open range then, with nothing fenced except a man's fields."

"Havin' a lawful fence meant you had a post every rod (16 feet) and at least three wires. Longhorns could crawl right on through a fence, an' knocked down more stuff than they ate. If you had a legal fence the stockmen would pay for damages, but only about half what they thought it was worth. Some ranchers would plant four or five rows of sorghum cane around a field, then if the cows got in, they would eat it and bloat.

"I remember that ol' wind blowin' out there most o' the time. ONE WAY for a few days, an' then BACK the OTHER way for a few days. One winter, a tall feller come ridin' into the yard, wearin' most of his suitcase under his sheepskin coat to stay warm. He was a tough ol' bird, so it didn't matter much. He had cattle out loose on the range and he was out lookin' for 'em. We had about two inches of fresh snow, an' I guess it was around 30 degrees below, an' the wind was blowin' hard. My dad, said to him, 'Ya' know, the snow never melts around here, it jest blows an' blows, back an' forth, 'till it finally gits all WORE OUT!'

"I started cowboyin' when I was seven years old, after my dad had an accident ridin' a thoroughbred horse after a rain. The horse slipped, fell and broke the old man's leg, those thoroughbred's bein' a little awkward on their feet anyways, they're more runners than stock horses. We had 385 head of cattle on open range and I looked after 'em, doing a man's work on the ranch with my dad crippled up and all, on crutches like he was.

"I remember havin' a Shetland then, one of the skinny kind, a track pony. He sure as the world had a mind of his own, as mean as he could be, usin' his teeth as well as kickin'. Mother couldn't saddle him on her own, and he liked to have killed me a couple o'times. I had a good quirt and spurs, so at times he did mind me purdy good.

"When my pony wasn't behavin' right, Dad would hobble out on his crutches an' crack 'im with his 'blacksnake,' an' snap a little hair out of 'im. He was really good with that whip, an' could snap the fuzz off a fly at fifteen feet! He had a nice, long one, not like the ones nowadays, an' he could really get a good snap out of it. I can still see that pony, squealin' an' rollin' around on the ground, but it was a good way to git 'im to mindin' for a few days.

"Even the horses was different back then, it seems. They were wilder, woolier, and a durn sight meaner to boot. Ya'd better git up travelin' fast when they throwed ya'. Them ol' horses would whirl around, go to lookin' for ya' an' hunt ya' down! We'd catch a bunch of them old range critters an' put 'em to work in the rodeo.

"I used to think I could ride anything that had hair and four legs, but there was one horse that nobody could ever stay on. Anybody who ever rode that stretch of Colorado, up into Montana, or over to the Dakotas, knows which one I'm talkin' about. He was a legendary 'piece of work' named Ol' Midnight. He went through his whole entire life pitchin' cowboys 'hind end over tea kettle' into the dust.

"Actually he was gentle, jest play actin', an' not a bit mean, when he wasn't showin' off at the rodeo. He would look over the crowd, wait for the rider to git a good seat, an' then when they opened that gate the Old Pro would come out like a hand grenade, an' you'd wonder where he went. They had a hundred dollars on him one year for anyone who could ride him. Nobody was able to ride him though, including me. The Ol' Rip Snorter was finally retired to the Wilbur, Washington area, at the age of thirty-two. He ended his days unridden, an' respected all the more.

"I was proud to be cowboyin' with the best of 'em. Talk about thick hides...those old hands had some great stories to tell. We seldom lost any cattle, but the work was purdy tough on both horses an' men. When a bunch o' fellas worked together like that, they'd git to braggin' on how they can ride this or rope that better'n the other feller, an' then they've have themselves a little friendly competition goin'.

"Most every Sunday, somebody would run in a bunch of range horses and we'd have a rodeo. The big ones were usually part of a fair or a Fourth of July celebration that might last a few days. I pro-rodeoed some, but never took home a championship buckle. I did make a bit of money at it. I might have stuck to it a little longer, if it hadn't a been for my 'missus-to-be.' I got to worryin' about 'er, frettin' about me while she was sittin' up there in the stands, chewin' her nails, so it seemed like it was easier, an' more fun, jest to git married!

"When I came to Idaho along with my wife, I became a 'Timber Beast,' tradin' cuttin' horses for cuttin' trees. That was B.C.—Before Chainsaws. There were a lot of Scandinavians an' Frenchmen workin' with me. They were good lumberjacks, fast on their feet an' 'catty,' but they didn't do much ridin'.

"Later on, I started shoein' horses. I picked up plenty from jest watchin', listenin', an' askin' questions in that order. Old Man Drier, who taught me, was the best blacksmith in town, no one could hold a hammer to 'im. If ya' gave 'im the right tools an' a piece of iron, he could fashion just about anything a feller needed, metalwise.

"I got to where I could hot shoe a horse or mule just right an' built up my own sort o' reputation because of it. Some of the mules were so mean, they'd just as soon kick you over the fence as look at you. One ol' pack mule never would stand for shoein'. You'd have to hog tie 'im an' slap the iron on while ya' had 'im on the ground.

"When you traveled maybe 200 miles or so, an' shoed 15 horses with the juice runnin' off ya', when it wasn't even rainin', ya' could call it a purdy good day! I probably shoed some 25,000 horses over the past forty years. Trimmin' an' shoein' sometimes as many as 23 head a day."

THE BANKER AND THE MAID

Traditional Melody
Arranged by Will McCain Clauson

Words by
Anthony Wayne Webner III

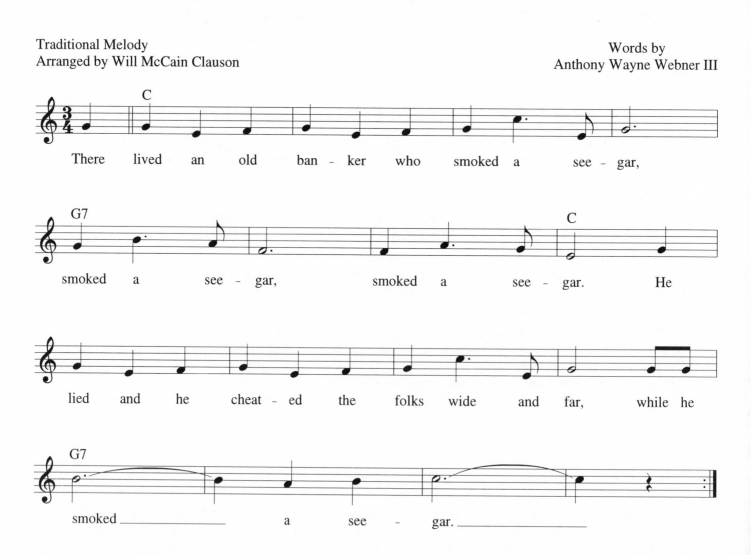

There lived an old ban - ker who smoked a see - gar, smoked a see - gar, smoked a see - gar. He lied and he cheat - ed the folks wide and far, while he smoked _____ a see - gar. _____

THE BANKER AND THE MAID

There lived an old banker who smoked a seegar.
Smoked a seegar, smoked a seegar.
He lied and he cheated the folks wide and far,
While he smoked a seegar.

In front of the bank stood a maid who sold flowers.
A maid who sold flowers, a maid who sold flowers,
In all kinds of weather through long weary hours,
She stood selling flowers.

On a day dark and dreary, she stood in the cold.
With no flowers sold, while the banker so bold,
Appraised this frail creature with beauty untold,
As she stood in the cold.

He called from the doorway, "Sweet lass, don't despair!
Why stand you there, in the cold frosty air?
There's nothing to fear, and I've comfort to share.
Sweet lass, don't despair!"

With silver and gold, he bought all that she had.
Once, the maid sad, was now, the maid glad.
Her sweet flowered youth, he then stole like a cad.
Stole like a cad!

She warmed by his fire, and he drew her near.
Dried every tear, called her his "Dear".
He promised her wealth and to wed in a year.
Wed in a year.

But the maid was betrayed for the banker had lied.
She sobbed and she sighed, in anguish she cried.
"He broke my dear heart!," then the maid up and died.
The poor maid, she died.

The maid is in heaven, with angels today.
They took her away, where golden harps play.
The banker's below with the devil to pay,
He's down there to stay.

My tale it has ended, my song now is done.
A moral, there's one, so listen, my son.
There's nothing in life you can truly bank on,
You're here and then you're gone.

> **FAULT FINDIN'**
> *When there's GOOD in the WORST of us,*
> *And BAD in the BEST of us,*
> *Why should ANY of US,*
> *Find fault with the REST of US!*
> **- Unknown**

THE BIG BRAHAMA BULL

Words Curley Fletcher

Music Arr. by Will Clauson

I was snap - pin' out broncs for the Ol' Fly - in',

"U" at for - ty a month like a good buck - a -

roo, when the boss comes a round an' he sez, "Ya' know,

Lad, ya' look pur - dy good ri - din' hor - ses that's

bad. Ya'___ see I ain't got no more out - laws to

break, But I'll buy ya', a tic - ket an' give ya' a

stake, at ta - min' the bad 'uns, well, You ain't so

slow, an' ya' might do some good at the big ro - de - o!"

THE BIG BRAHAMA BULL

I was snappin' out broncos for the Ol' Flyin' "U",
At forty a month, like a good buckaroo;
When the boss comes around an' he sez, "Ya' know, Lad,
Ya' look purdy good ridin' horses that's bad.
Ya' see, I ain't got no more outlaws to break,
But I'll buy ya' a ticket an' give ya' a stake,
At tamin' the bad 'uns, well, ya ain't so slow,
An ya' might do some good at the big ro—de—o.

Jes' lay off the likker an' don't ya' git full,
An' think ya' kin ride that ol' Big Brahama Bull.
He's bad as they make 'em, an' don't ya' forget,
He's throw'd a lotta riders, he ain't bin rode yet.
So I packs up my war bags an' starts raisin' dust,
I'm huntin' that show an' the big bull to bust.
I enters the contest an' pays 'em my fee,
An' tells 'em t'look at a twister, that's me!

While they wuz puttin' the bull in the chutes,
I wuz bucklin' m'spurs to the heels of m'boots.
I looks the brute over, an' to m'surprise,
There's a foot an' a half in between his two eyes.
On top of his withers he packs a big hump,
I cinches my riggin' in back of that lump.
I lights in the middle an' lets out a scream,
As he flies out a bellerin', the rest's a bad dream.

He hits fer the East, but he lits in the West,
I'm hangin' on tight, doin' my level best.
He dips down so low that my boots fill with dirt,
He's a poppin' the buttons right off o' m'shirt.
His horns are a-tossin', I'm hurtin' behind,
My neck gits a-crackin', I sorter goes blind.
The bull's barrel turnin' way up in the air,
An' he leaves me a-sittin' on nuthin' up there.

As I turns over, below I kin see
He's pawin' the ground, jes' waitin' fer me.
I pitchurs a grave an' a big slab o' wood
Sayin', "Here lies a twister that thought he wuz good."
When I hits the dirt boys, I had enough sense
T' outrun that bull through a hole in the fence.
I dives through that hole, an' I want ya' t' know
I ain't goin' back t' no wild Ro—de—o!

> It's TOO LATE to SHUT the GATE
> when the HORSE is GONE.
> **- Will McCain Clauson**

97

THE BOTTLE SHACK
(Little Brown Jug)

New Words by
Will McCain Clauson

Trad. Arr. by
Will McCain Clauson

My jug and I live all a - lone, in a bot - tle shack we
made me loose my wife and home, a lit - tle brown jug is

call our home, Built with bot - tles of gin and rum,
all I own, And a bot - tle shack near the rail - road track where I

That's where we have all our fun. (You) Ha - Ha - Ha,
fall down drunk on a slee - pin rack.

you and me, We're as hap - py as can be.

Ha - Ha - Ha, you and I, Fill me up on corn and rye!

THE BOTTLE SHACK
(Little Brown Jug)

My jug and I live all alone,
In a bottle shack we call our home.
Built with bottles of gin and rum,
That's where we have all our fun.

You made me lose my wife and home,
A little brown jug is all I own,
And a bottle shack, near the railroad track,
Where I fall down drunk on a sleepin' rack.

Chorus:
Ha-Ha-Ha, you and me.
We're as happy as can be.
Ha-Ha-Ha, you and I,
Fill me up on corn and rye!

A bottle shack is what we share,
It's my new home, it's free from care.
From our shack, no need to roam,
For where you're at is home, sweet home!

When I need a drop, your cork I pull,
I'm happy to see you fat and full.
If you were a lake and I was a duck,
I'd paddle around and drink you up!

Repeat chorus

This bottled shack is nice and warm,
It keeps us from the cold and storm.
When the wind comes howlin' 'round,
It makes a happy whistlin' sound.

With a chug-a-lug, your cork I pull,
You little brown jug, you fill me full.
I lift you up right near to my nose,
Tip you over, and down it goes.

Repeat chorus

I have no friends, I've lost them all,
My love for you was my downfall,
You gave my nose this purple hue,
In spite of all, I still love you!

One day I left my bottle shack,
With my little brown jug packed in a sack
I stubbed my toe, and down I fell,
And thought I'd broke the jug to pieces.

New chorus:
No. No. No., it wasn't true.
Ha-Ha-Ha, I still had you.
Ha-Ha-Ha you and me,
We're as happy as can be.

Repeat chorus

Ha-Ha-Ha you and me,
We're as happy as can be.
Ha-Ha-Ha, you and I,
Fill me up on corn and rye!

I'm happy as a bug in a rug,
When I'm with you, my little brown jug
I'll live with you in the bottle shack,
Where you won't run away, and never come back!

Repeat chorus
(Try making up some new verses yourself.)

Carl Sandburg said, "Early settlers in the West found that log cabins were more scarce as the timber thinned out on the way westward. A Sod House was the easiest to set up. First, the cellar was dug, then long slices of turf were placed around the cellar lines, and the sod roof was held up by wooden cross poles."

The early pioneers were most inventive. They did, indeed, have shacks built from the many bottles to be found in the vicinity of the saloon. I've adapted the tune of "Little Brown Jug" to tell you some more about the bottle shacks.

*This page has been
left blank to avoid
awkward page turns*

THE COLORADO TRAIL

Words and Music Arr. by
Will McCain Clauson

Eyes like the mor - nin' star, Cheeks like a rose. Lau - ra is a pur - dy gal, God Al - migh - ty knows. Weep, rain's a - fal - lin' now, Wail, winds, _____ wail. All a - long, a - long, a - long the Co - lo - ra - do trail.

THE COLORADO TRAIL

Eyes like the mornin' star,
Cheeks like a rose.
Laura is a purdy gal,
God Almighty knows.

Weep, rain's a-fallin' now,
Wail, winds, wail,
All along, along, along,
The Colorado trail.

Lips like berries growin' wild,
Kisses sweet as wine.
Laura is a purdy gal,
Someday, she'll be mine.

Weep, rain's a-fallin' now,
Wail, winds, wail,
All along, along, along,
The Colorado trail.

–2nd verse by W.M.C.

Colorado may be pronounced with a long "a" as in Colo - ray - do. This is undoubtedly one of Carl Sandburg's favorite cowboy songs. When we'd have a "git together" with others, I remember him always singing this song, often unaccompanied (sometimes more than once in the course of an evening) as if he were out, all alone on the trail.

The Horse / Riding

"The West had no written histories, no songs, no legends until the horse became a part of the lives of the Indians and the pioneer settlers. A whole new world was founded from the horse's back."

- Bradley Smith

Horses were introduced to the Americas by the Spanish. From the few mounts they brought with them, came the huge bands of Mustangs that transformed the West. Animals abandoned by early explorers, or those that strayed from ranches or missions, mixed with the Spanish mounts that escaped, were lost or stolen. Thus, the horse began its phenomenal spread across the west.

The Spanish arrived in Mexico with 553 men and 16 horses. When they landed on the coast of New Spain, it was the horses that conquered Mexico. The Aztec warriors continued to fight even against cannon, until the horsemen appeared. Montezuma's warriors fled from the armored and mounted Spaniards, thinking that man and animal were one supernatural being.

Six of the first horses brought to New Spain were mares, and these and others that followed produced the offspring that populated North and South America. Arabian horses first arrived in the Americas with the Spanish conquistadors, and are now found on many a modern ranch.

Indians began stealing horses from the Spaniards. DeSoto lost many of his horses near the Mississippi.

Northern Indians such as the Blackfeet and Sioux would travel thousands of miles south in order to obtain their first horses. The Cheyenne stole the first pintos and became known as the Painted Horsed People. Appaloosas (Mongolian horses brought to Spain by the Moors) were stolen by the Nez Perce and bred for war horses. Snake Indians called the first horses Big Dogs or Medicine Dogs. To the Blackfeet they were known as Elk dogs.

Pintos were valued by the Indians because of their bright colors: a white spot on the horse could show the Indian's bloody hand print to denote that he was on the warpath. Appaloosas were favored for their intelligence, stamina and colorful markings. The Nez Perce bred only their best Appaloosas, either gelding or trading the horses they deemed inferior.

Thoroughbreds, although aristocrats in the horse world, were rare in the West in the nineteenth century, primarily used for racing in such western towns as Denver, San Francisco and Sacramento. They were not often used as cow horses, unless a horse was less than one-half Thoroughbred.

Quarter horses are aptly named "AMERICA'S BREED." They were first bred in colonial Carolina and Virginia by mixing English Sires (thoroughbred Studs of Barb lineage) with native Mares (Spanish-Indian Dams).

The quarter horse is the favorite of the American cowboy. They were bred for short bursts of speed and the ability to cut an animal from the herd. They are unparalleled for rapid speed, "cow sense," and agility. They stop and turn easily at the slightest command, and respond quickly to signals given with the rider's knees or posture.

Western riding evolved from four main branches: the Moorish warrior, who invaded and conquered the Southern part of Spain; the Native Americans; the U.S. Cavalry, and the Spanish horseman. Tack similar to ours was used on work and war horses even then.

The American Indians were amazing horsemen and had one of the finest light cavalries the world has ever known. They used a single rein and mostly rode bareback. Sometimes they would use a strap over the horse, to hook their toe into so they could lean over to shoot buffalo from under the horse's neck or to protect themselves from enemy fire. They would mount on either side of the horse and even jump on him from the back with remarkable dexterity.

The Cowman spent most of his time in the saddle, necessitating a broader seat and cantle. Although American saddles did not have a high horn, Mexican saddles usually did. They also had a larger top on the horn for dallying (to secure the reata, a braided rawhide rope) and to keep it from slipping off. The horns were made of brass, silver, rawhide, or sometimes even out of wood.

The Mexican cowboy always had a very long rope so they could let slack off if they needed to, although sometimes with disastrous results. If the rope slipped off the saddle horn while holding a steer, the dallyman's finger(s) could be taken off. American cowboys used a shorter rope, 25-30 feet, and tied it hard and fast to the horn, to help eliminate this.

HOME

A world of strife SHUT OUT, a world of love SHUT IN.
A place where the small are GREAT, and the great are SMALL.

🐎 🐎 🐎 🐎 🐎 🐎 🐎 🐎 🐎 🐎

SALT yer life with HUMOR,
PEPPER it with WIT,
SPICE it up with lots o' LOVE,
T' make the MOST o' IT!

- Will McCain Clauson

A COW TOWN
Twenty saloons an' a tin pie-anner,
A gal or two in a calico gown,
Three card Monte, an' shots of red eye,
All together they make a cow town.
-Anon.

THE DAYS OF THE FORTY-NINE

Traditional Words

Music by
Will McCain Clauson

You are ga - zin' now on Ol' Tom Moore, A re - lic of by - gone days. 'Tis a bum - mer now they call me, _____ But what care I for praise! It's oft, says I, for _____ days gone by, oh, it's oft I do re - pine for days of old, When we dug out gold, in the days of the for - ty - nine.

THE DAYS OF THE FORTY-NINE

You are gazin' now on Ol' Tom Moore,
A relic of bygone days.
'Tis a bummer now they call me,
But what care I for praise!
It's oft, says I, for days gone by,
Oh, it's oft I do repine,
For days of old,
When we dug out gold,
In the days of the forty-nine.

My comrades all, they loved me well,
That saucy, jolly crew.
A few hard cases I'll admit,
Though they were brave and true.
What e'er the punch, they ne'er would flinch,
Or would they fret or whine,
Like good ol' bricks,
They could stand the kicks,
In the days of the forty-nine.
Like good ol' bricks,
They could stand those kicks,
In the days of forty-nine.

Nathan Howard "Jack" Thorpe

In 1889, Jack Thorpe spent a year covering one thousand five hundred miles on horseback throughout New Mexico and Texas collecting songs. He was a pioneer in this field, as his was the first book of its kind. He had the foresight to see that the songs were going to become lost to future generations. His was the groundwork that was to be the foundation for latter day collectors and singers.

At the end of the year long trip he had more than enough material to publish a song book but there was no interest shown in the project by publishers of the period. He decided to publish the work himself in 1908 at the printer's cost of 35 cents a book!

He claimed, jokingly, that in fifty years of living in the West he had never heard a cowboy sing. This seems contradictory as he prefaces each of the songs collected with "I heard this song sung in... and by...." The melodies were not annotated in his book.

THE FOOZLE
The biggest foozle I ever did see,
Was a man that lived in Tennessee,
He put his shirt on over his coat,
and buttoned his trousers around his throat.
- Unknown

THE GAL I LEFT BEHIND ME

Traditional Irish Melody

Words and Music Arr. by
Will McCain Clauson

Oh, I can't for - get the night we met, The star - lit sky a - bove me, an' the moon - beams sent their sil - v'ry light, When she first vowed to love me. The ___ vows we made that star - ry night, will al - ways cheer and bind me, to be faith - ful to the gal I love. The gal I left be - hind me. That sweet lit - tle gal, that true lit - tle gal, with me dar - lin' soon' you'll find me, with the gal I gave my true love to, the gal I left be - hind me.

THE GAL I LEFT BEHIND ME

Oh, I can't forget the night we met,
The moonlit sky above me,
And the moonbeams sent their silv'ry light,
When first she vowed to love me.

The vows we made that starry night,
Will always cheer and bind me,
To be faithful to the gal I love,
The gal I left behind me.

Chorus:
That sweet little gal, that true little gal,
With me darlin' soon you'll find me,
With the gal I gave my true love to,
The gal I left behind me.

I struck the trail in sixty-nine,
The herd strung out behind me,
As I rode along, my mind ran back,
To the gal I left behind me.

Oh, the wind did blow, and the rain did flow,
And the hail did fall and blind me,
But in my thoughts, she'd always be,
The gal I left behind me.

Repeat Chorus

If ever I get off the trail,
And the In-*die*-ans don't find me,
I'll make my way straight back again,
To the gal I left behind me.

I'll take her in my arms once more,
'Neath the starry skies above me,
That sweet little gal, that true little gal,
The gal that vowed to love me.

Repeat Chorus

SLEEPIN' IN
In a soft feather bed,
I wuz sleepin'-in.
With silky-white sheets
Pulled up t' my chin.
When the boss cries,
"Time t' git up now, Jim."
An' I wakes t' find,
I WUZ DREAMIN' AGIN.
- Will McCain Clauson

THE GREAT GRANDFOLKS

Words by Anthony Wayne Webner III

Music by Will McCain Clauson

THE GREAT GRANDFOLKS

The Great Grandfolks in days of old,
Were Pioneers and Pilgrims bold.
The "Elephant" they went to see,
The Great Grand West so wild and free.

In prairie schooners long and tall,
The Great Grandfolks they packed it all.
Their kith and kin and all their gear,
Their dreams, their schemes, their hopes and fears.

Chorus:
The Great Grandfolks made the Great Grand trek,
Though the way was hard they ne'er looked back.
With Great Grand faith in God's Grand Plan,
The Great Grandfolks sought* the "promised land".

(Cross) desert sands and grassy plains,
Flowed endless streams of wagon trains.
They made their way o'er rivers wide,
To the milk and honey on the side.

With buffalo grass they built their home,
With bricks of sod and prairie foam,
And sheltered there 'gainst the winds and rains,
They settled there on the Western plains.

Chorus

The Great Grandfolks, when their kids were young,
Barred their door with a wagon's tongue,
And kept them safe and raised them strong,
Taught 'em sums and psalms and right from wrong.

With Great Grand strength they made a stand,
'gainst the wilderness and the savage land.
For ne'er faint heart could win the West,
The Great Grandfolks, they stood the test.

Chorus

The great Grandfolks had a Great Grand dream,
Of a Great Grand nation like ya' never seen,
A Great Grand land stretched from sea to sea,
For Great Grand folks like you and me.

Chorus

change to: "found" *in chorus # two;*
"built" *in chorus # three and four*

THE LOVELY OHIO

Additional Words by
Will McCain Clauson

Trad. Melody Arr. and Adapted by
Will McCain Clauson

Come all you brisk young fel - lers ____ who have a mind to roam, ____ All
in some fo - reign coun - te - ree, a long way from home, ____ All
in some fo - reign coun - te - ree a - long with me to go, ____ To
set - tle on the banks of the love - ly O - hi - o, ____ To
set - tle on the banks of the love - ly O - hi - o. ____ Come

---

BEIN' NOSEY
When folks dont't MIND their BUSINESS,
Mos' likely you will find,
They probl'ly got no BUSINESS,
Er else ain't got no MIND.
- Unknown - Edited W M C

THE LOVELY OHIO

Come all you brisk young fellers who have a mind to roam,
All in some foreign count-te-ree, a long way from home,
All in some foreign count-te-ree along with me to go,
To settle on the banks of the lovely Ohio,
To settle on the banks of the lovely Ohio.

Come all you buxom fair young maids who have a mind to go,
To see a foreign count-te-ree, come, maidens, Westward Ho!
To see a foreign count-te-ree where you can knit and sew,
And settle on the banks of the lovely Ohio,
And settle on the banks of the lovely Ohio.

Come all you lads and lassies, the land we'll reap and mow,
And build a cabin in the woods, down by the river's flow,
We'll build a cabin in the woods and watch our fam'ly grow,
We'll settle on the banks of the lovely Ohio,
We'll settle on the banks of the lovely Ohio.

A NEW DAY

What if T'MORROW never comes
When YESTERDAYS are gone?

One DAY, lived well, is worth livin';
it gives ya' HOPE t'move on.

HOPE is free, don't cost a cent;
why worry 'long the way?

The FUTURE's the first light
of a bright NEW DAY.

-Will McCain Clauson

MY WISH FOR YOU
(A favorite poem of Charlie Russell)

May your DAYS be better than the best you've had.
Your WRINKLES from laughs, not frowns.
May your NIGHTS bring dreams that make you glad,
And your JOYS be mountains, not mounds.

-Author Unknown

The HUMAN animal is the ONLY one that can be skinned twice.
                                                    - Anonymous

THE OLD CHISHOLM TRAIL

Trad. Arr.
Additional Words by Will McCain Clauson

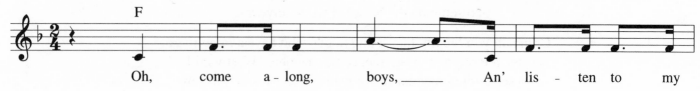

Oh, come a – long, boys, _____ An' lis – ten to my

tale. Tell ya' 'bout my trou – bles on the old Chis – holm

Chorus

Trail. Come a ki – yi yip – py, yip – py yay, yip – py

yay. Come a ki – yi yip – py, yip – py yay!

THE OLD CHISHOLM TRAIL

Oh, come along boys,
An' listen to my tale.
Tell ya 'bout my troubles,
On the old Chisholm Trail.

Chorus:
Come a ki-yi yippy, yippy yay, yippy yay.
Come a ki-yi-yippy, yippy yay.

or:
Come a ki-yi yip, yippy yay, yippy yay
Come a ki-yi yip, yippy yay.

We started up the trail.
October twenty third.
Started up the trail,
With the "Two U" herd.

(cont.)
Chorus

I brought along my dog,
I raised 'im from a pup.
He could stand on his hind legs,
If you'd hold the front ones up.

Chorus

The work was hard,
And the steers was mean.
The boss was tough,
And the pay was lean.

Chorus

We're up in the saddle,
Before daylight.
Before we sleep,
The moon shines bright.

Chorus

Woke up one morning,
On the old Chisholm Trail.
Rope in m' hand,
And a cow by the tail.

Chorus

I went to the boss
To draw my roll.
He had me figured out,
Ten dollars in the hole.

Chorus

So the boss and me,
We had a little chat.
Then I hit him in the face,
With my old slouch hat.

Chorus

The Old Chisholm Trail, a famous cattle trail which ran from San Antonio, Texas to Abilene, Kansas, was named after Jesse Chisholm (pronounced 'Chizzum') a Cherokee Indian trader. It is claimed that the above song had more than a thousand verses, and they sang them all the way from San Antonio to Abilene.

THE PIGGY BANK
If ya' DON'T save yer PENNY,
You'll never have ANY.
But they'll GROW into MANY...
If the PIG gits the PENNY.
- Will McCain Clauson

THE OLD MAN AND HIS WIFE

Words and Music Arr. by
Will McCain Clauson

Traditional

THE OLD MAN AND HIS WIFE

There was an old man that lived in the woods,
As you can plainly see,
That swore he could do more work in a day,
Than his wife could do in three.
"If that be so," the old woman said,
"Then this you must allow,
That you should do my work for a day,
While I will drive the plow."

(cont.)

But first you must milk the tiny cow,
For fear she should go dry.
And then you must feed the little pigs,
That are within the sty.
And then you must watch the speckled hen,
'Lest she should lay away.
And you must wind the reel of twine,
That I spun yesterday.

The old woman took the staff in her hand,
And went to drive the plough.
The old man took the pail in his hand,
And went to milk the cow.
But Tiny hinched and Tiny flinched,
And Tiny cocked her nose.
And Tiny gave the old man such a kick,
That the blood ran to his toes.

'twas "Here my good cow" and "Whoa, my good cow,"
And "Now my good cow, stand still.
If ever I milk this cow again,
It will be against my will."
And when he'd milked the tiny cow,
For fear she should go dry,
Why then he went to feed the pigs,
That were within the sty.

But as he came into the sty,
To give the pigs their hire,
They all ran in between his legs,
And threw him in the mire.
And as he watched the speckled hen,
Lest she should lay away,
He clean forgot the reel of yarn,
That his wife spun yesterday.

When the old man's wife came home that night,
She laughed and was quite glad,
To find him in such a terrible plight,
And lookin' so glum and sad.
He swore by all the leaves on the tree,
And all the stars in Heaven,
That she could do more work in a day,
Than he could do in seven.

COMPATIBILITY
Before ya' run in DOUBLE-harness...
git t' know the OTHER horse.
- Will McCain Clauson

THE OL' GRAY MARE

Traditional Melody

* Additional Words by
Will McCain Clauson

* Second, third, fourth, fifth verses - original by Will McCain Clauson

116

THE OL' GRAY MARE

The Ol' Gray Mare, she ain't what she used to be,
Ain't what she used to be,
Ain't what she used to be,
The Ol' Gray Mare, she ain't what she used to be,
Many long years ago.

Many long years ago.
Many long years ago.
The Ol' Gray Mare, she ain't what she used to be,
Ain't what she used to be,
Ain't what she used to be,
The Ol' Gray Mare, she ain't what she used to be,
Many long years ago.

*We'd hitch 'er up and go for a buggy ride,
Go for a buggy ride,
Go for a buggy ride,
We'd hitch 'er up and go for a buggy ride,
Many long years ago.

Many long years ago,
Many long years ago,
We'd hitch 'er up and go for a buggy ride,
Go for a buggy ride,
Go for a buggy ride,
We'd hitch 'er up and go for a buggy ride,
Many long years ago.

(Use above pattern for the following verses:)

*The Ol' Gray Mare, she ain't trottin' 'round no more.
She's gone where the good mares go

*The Ol' Gray Mare, she sat on the whiffle tree.
She broke the thing in two!

*We're ridin' 'round in a horseless carriage now.
The Ol' Gray Mare, is gone

* Original WMC

Whiffle tree - a wooden bar that is single bolted on the shaft.
A whiffle tree is used on a single horse buggy.
Shaft - fastened to the harness, goes on each side of the horse, and is held up in front by a breast collar.
Horseless carriage - early day name for an automobile.

NUTHIN'
DON'T WORRY 'bout NUTHIN'.
NUTHIN'S gonna turn out right anyways.
"NUTHIN' ever DUZ. DON'T WORRY!"
- Source Arlene Giles

THE QUILTIN' PARTY

Trad. Words and Melody

Arr. Will McCain Clauson

The Old West: When men were men and wimmen knew it.
- Frank Lomonaco

THE QUILTIN' PARTY

In the sky the bright stars glittered,
On the bank the pale moon shone.
It was from Aunt Dinah's quiltin' party,
I was seein' Nellie home,
I was seein' Nellie home,
I was seein' Nellie home.
It was from Aunt Dinah's quiltin' party,
I was seein' Nellie home.

On my arm a soft hand rested,
Rested light as ocean foam.
It was from Aunt Dinah's quiltin' party,
I was seein' Nellie home,
I was seein' Nellie home,
I was seein' Nellie home.
It was from Aunt Dinah's quiltin' party,
I was seein' Nellie home.

Tips for the Tenderfoot

Think of the hoss as yer friend, but always approach 'em cautiously from the front, preferably "talkin' some to 'em." Curry 'em with a gentle hand. For the hoss's comfort, learn to use a saddle blanket correctly, always smoothin' it out so's it ain't got no wrinkles. Put yer saddle on next, makin' sure that some joker ain't slipped a burr under it! (Cowboys were known to do things like that).

CINCHIN' yer saddle: If yer hoss starts bloatin' as yer cinchin', as some of 'em do, jest give 'em a good thump in the belly with yer knee an' he'll slim down real fast-like. That's the time to cinch 'em up quick, but not TOO tight cuz he could end up gittin' cinch sore, or worse, he might like to start buckin'. Ride a bit an' then tighten it up a little if ya' need to.

GITTIN' on: Mount on the left side, aware of the fact that the hoss can only see you out of his left eye. If ya' don't know left from right, jes git on an' see what happens! (OH NO, ya' better not try that, yer hoss might not be used to it.) Grip the reins an' the hoss's mane with yer left hand, put yer left foot in the stirrup an' grab the cantle with yer right hand. When ya' lift up, throw yer right leg over the hoss's rump, ease down gently in the saddle an' slip your right foot in the stirrup.

STARTIN' up: Face the hoss in the direction ya' wanna go—that way if you don't get there, ya' can blame it on yer hoss. Squeeze both yer legs 'ginst the hoss's sides an' let the reins follow the movin' of the hoss's head. Don't look at yer hoss, but maybe his ears (cuz they might tell ya' somethin'), keep yer eyes on where yer gonna.

If yer usin' yer legs to control the hoss, an' ya' wanna go RIGHT—press yer LEFT leg 'ginst the hoss; if ya' wanna go LEFT—press yer RIGHT leg 'ginst the hoss. If yer using yer reins to control 'em, lay the RIGHT rein 'ginst the hoss's neck to go LEFT—an' lay the LEFT rein 'ginst the neck if ya' wanna go RIGHT.

BACKIN': Squeeze both reins even-like, without lettin' the hoss go forwards. Then, squeeze both legs 'ginst the sides of the hoss. If he don't back up, he ain't workin' right.

STOPPIN': Sit further back in the saddle an' lightly squeeze yer fingers together on the reins (don't tug 'em to hard, or ya'll be going back t'where you came from!).

GITTIN' off: Make sure the hoss is standin' still. To git off: Jes' go back to GITTIN' ON, but then do it all backwards.

GROOMIN': A hoss likes to be curried, 'specially after a long ride, but ya' kin do this before ya' saddle up, too, if ya' want. When ya' remove yer saddle, wipe 'im to git the sweat off, usin' the backside of a curry comb. If ya' ain't got one, a wad of hay will do. After that, walk 'im a bit to cool 'im down.

On the trail, don't forget yer hoss does a purdy good job of groomin' himself. Don't let his rollin' around on the ground startle you, he's jes' takin' care of hisself the nat'ral way an' usually gits up with a smooth, shiny coat.

Don't tie a hoss up hard an' fast by the bridle reins, use a halter. If there ain't nuthin' to tie yer hoss to, ya' kin always dig a hole an' put the loop of the halter in it, cover it up, an' tamp it down. If ya' hobble yer hoss he might still walk down the road a bit anyway if ya' don't shorten 'em up enough.

After the first day on the trail, 'specially if yer a "Dude" or it's been a rough trail, ya' might have'ta eat yer chili standin' up, as yer wonderin' how anythin' stuffed with hay could be so hard.

If yer gonna be closely associated with yer horse, give 'em a name, if he ain't got one that ya' know of, an' call him such. On a drive a hoss will travel at least twice as far as a cow so you have to change hoss's a few times a day. Cutting out a new hoss is a job of the wrangler.

THE RAILROAD CORRAL

Words by Joseph Mills Hanson (1900)

Trad. Arr. and Adapt.
Will McCain Clauson

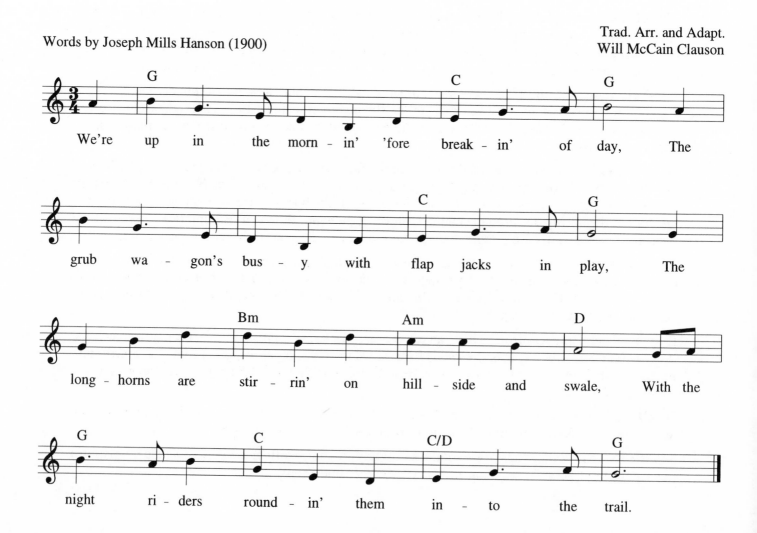

THE RAILROAD CORRAL

We're up in the mornin' 'fore breakin' of day,
The grub wagon's busy with flap jacks in play,
The long horns are stirrin' on hillside and swale,
With the night riders roundin' them into the trail.

Take up your cinches,
And shake up your reins!
Wake up your bronco,
And break for the plains!
Come, roust them red steers from the long chaparral,
The outfit is off for the railroad corral!

The sun circles upward, the steers as they plod,
Are poundin' to powder the hot prairie sod.
Oh, it seems, as the dust turns you dizzy and sick,
That you'll never reach noon and the cool, shady crick.

Tie up your kerchief,
And ply up your nag!
Dry up your grumbles,
And try not to lag!
Come, larrup them steers from the long chaparral,
We're far on the way to the railroad corral!

The afternoon shadows are startin' to fall,
And an ol' mud stuck maverick is startin' to bawl.
You've been ridin' drag; eatin' dust as if flies,
Now you've drawn ridin' night herd 'til dawn breaks the skies

Shake out your rawhide,
Snake it up fair!
Break your ol' bronco,
To takin' his share!
Come, now for the steers in the long chaparral,
It's all in the drive to the railroad corral!

But the longest of days must reach evenin' at last,
When the hills are all climbed and the creeks are all passed.
And, the tired herd droops in the yellowin' light,
Let 'em loaf if they will, for the railroad's in sight

Flap up your holster,
Snap up your belt!
Strap up your saddle,
Whose lap you have felt!
Goodbye to them steers and the long chaparral,
There's a town that's a trump by the railroad corral!

THE STERN OLD BACHELOR

Source: Howard "Chip" Culver

Arranged and Adapted by
Will McCain Clauson

I am a stern old bach - e - lor, ___ my age is six - ty four. ___ I do de - clare. I'll nev - er flirt ___ with wim-men an - y more! _____ When I come home late at night, ___ I smile and walk right in. _____ There's no one wait - in' at the door ___ with a great big roll - in' pin. _____

THE STERN OLD BACHELOR

I am a stern old bachelor,
My age is sixty four.
I do declare, I'll never flirt,
With wimmen any more!

When I come home late at night,
I smile and walk right in.
There's no one waiting at the door,
With a great big rollin' pin.

(cont.)

I go to bed when I well please,
I get up just the same.
I change my socks three times a year,
With no one to complain.

At night, when I'm asleep in bed,
My snores they do no harm.
I never have to walk the floor
With an infant in my arms.

When I die and go to heaven,
As all good bachelors do,
I'll never have to grieve or fear,
My wife won't get there too.

I'll stay a stern old bachelor,
On that you can rely.
I'll stay a stern old bachelor,
Until the day I die.

O'REILLY IS DEAD
(Sing to the tune of "Irish Washerwoman")

*O'Reilly is dead,
And O'Reely don't know it.
O'Reely is dead,
And O'Reilly don't know it.
They're both lyin' dead,
In the very same bed.
So, neither one knows,
That the other is dead!*

- Unknown

RESTIN'

*I wish I wuz a little rock,
Jes' a'settin' on a hill.
Doin' nuthin' all day long,
But jes' a'settin' still.*

*I wouldn't eat, I wouldn't drink.
I wouldn't even worsh,
I'd SET up there a HUNDRED years,
An' REST myself, by gorsh.*

-Anonymous

THE STREETS OF LAREDO
(The Cowboy's Lament)

New Words by
Anthony Wayne Webner III

Music Arr. and Adapted
Will McCain Clauson

THE STREETS OF LAREDO
(The Cowboy's Lament)

As I walked on the streets of Laredo,
As I walked in Laredo one day,
I spied a young cowboy all wrapped in white linen.
Wrapped in white linen as cold as the clay.

"Kind friend, will you lend me an ear for the hearin',"
His voice whispered softly, the words drew me nigh.
"Come sit down beside me and hear my sad story,
I'm done in the breast, and I know I must die."

"Oh, once in the saddle, I used to go dashin',
Hoorahin' 'n' sportin'," the cowboy did say,
"And pleasured I've been by the liquor and ladies.
And sadly I'm seein' it all pass away."

"So, beat the drum slowly. and play the fife lowly,
And sound 'The Dead March' as you carry me 'long,
Oh, lay my head down 'neath the sod of the prairie,
For I'm a young cowboy and know I've done wrong."

"Find a brace of white horses for pullin' my coffin.
Find six lonely riders for bearin' my pall.
Set the ladies that pleasured, to walkin' behind me,
A'weepin' and wailin', bemoanin' my fall."

"Oh, blanket my grave bed with sweet smellin' blossoms,
Fresh picked of the prairies I no more shall roam.
And 'The Psalm of the Shepherd', read softly above me,
Just say on my marker, 'This Cowboy's Gone Home'."

In a trough of clear water I dipped my bandanna,
And wet his cold lips as I cradled his head.
With a sigh and shudder, his soul then departed,
On the streets of Laredo the cowboy lay dead.

So, they beat the drum slowly, and played the fife lowly,
And sounded "Death's March" as they carried him home.
The cowboy, he's gone from the shadowy valley,
Bound for green pastures, forever to roam.

THE RACE

All must run the race of life,
What matters ain't the pace.
What counts most, when life is done,
Is HOW ya' RAN the RACE.

If ya' lost, an' still kin smile,
An' done the BEST ya' can,
Ya' kin take a bow, my friend,
Ya' PROVED that yer A MAN.

WHO'S THERE?

I say my pray'rs, an' go to church,
With the Lord I often visit.
When it's time to climb them Golden Stairs,
He won't have to ask, "WHO IS IT?"
When I arrive at them Purly Gates,
No need to stand there...HOPIN',
I'll jes' knock, and then He'll say,
"COME IN, MY SON, IT'S OPEN!"

-Howard "Chip" Culver

THE YELLOW ROSE OF TEXAS

Arr. by Will McCain Clauson

Music by Col. Morgan (?)

1. There's a Yel - low Rose of Tex - as, That I am goin' to
2. She's the sweet - est Rose of col - or, This fel - la ev - er

see, No oth - er fel - la knows her, None
knew, Her eyes are bright as dia - monds, They

o - ther on - ly me, She ___ cried so when I
spar - kle like the dew, You may talk a - bout your

left her, It like to broke my heart, And ___
dear - est, And sing of Ro - sa Lee, But the

if I ev - er find her, We ___ nev - er more will part.
Yel - low Rose of Tex - as, Beats the belles of Ten - nes - see.

Language of the Old West

The Western Pioneers created a most colorful "language" uniquely their own, rich in metaphors, similes, and embellishments. It was fanciful, imaginative, at times exaggerated, but always to the the point, without wasting a word.

The spoken word begins as a desire to communicate an idea. That desire must be sufficiently large enough to propel the thinker to interaction, thereby uttering verbal sounds. The forming of these sounds does not necessarily mean communication and understanding will follow unless the person addressed also has an understanding of the vernacular.

Words and colloquialisms, while unrecognizable to the outsider, are very important to the process of communication in every culture in the world. The language of the Old West was no exception.

Words, and our varying degrees of intelligence separate us from the "world of the critter." It was of utmost importance in the Early West to educate; "the word was heard," and many new ones created to add to our Western speech. But "seein' it," in book form (words, paragraphs and sentences), was necessary.

For a people to continue to develop, the spoken word must be followed by the written word. Noah Webster was fully aware of this necessity, and the lack of it out West. He set about putting together a spelling book for a population that was to be self-taught, for the most part, or else remain illiterate.

Eight or ten thousand words became familiar to the eye and the bright youth, or earnest student, no matter what the age, could acquire the art of "readin' with a little help from others." His "spellin' book" became the most used school book in America in the early decades of the 19th century.

In the Old West, words were just "passed around" and "handed down," most of them not being learned at school. "The folks just made them up when they needed a good way of saying something." If the words turned out to be useful, other folks started using them as well as colloquial expressions. And later on, even old Noah used the most common ones in his dictionary.

In 1880, Thomas Edison coined a brand new word, all his own, "Hello." It was a surprise to me that it only first appeared in literature when Mark Twain described the first telephone operators as "Hello Girls." It wasn't until the year 1883 that the word was even published in an Oxford English dictionary.

Abraham Lincoln had an extraordinary power to make himself understood. It became a passion with him to "put all I have to say into words that cannot be misunderstood." In 1858, he said of a debating opponent that the only way you could make him quit talking would be to "STOP HIS MOUTH WITH A CORN COB."

"I do the very best I know how; the very best I can; and I mean to keep doing so until the end. If the end brings me out all right, what is said against me won't amount to anything. If the end brings me out wrong, ten angels swearing I was right would make no difference." **-Abraham Lincoln**

Stonewall Jackson used the expression "INSTANT IN PRAYER" and upon being asked what he meant, replied, "I have so fixed the habit, that I NEVER raise a glass of water to my lips without a moment's asking of God's blessing. I NEVER seal a letter without putting a word of prayer under the seal. I NEVER take a letter from the post without a brief sending of my thoughts heavenward. I think I can say that my "INSTANT IN PRAYER" is as fixed a HABIT as breathing."

In an encounter in the Civil War, the untrained troops under General Grant were hemmed in by the enemy. One of the officers rode in with the news, "We are surrounded." "Well," said Grant, "if that is so, we must CUT OUR WAY OUT as we CUT OUR WAY IN. We have WHIPPED them once, and we can do it again." His confidence quickly inspired his command and the troops took heart. They DID "CUT THEIR WAY OUT," they "WHIPPED AGAIN," and also went on to a series of brilliant victories.

Cowboy's Way of Speaking

*Git to know in advance
what he's gonna be talkin' 'bout,
then ya' don't have to pay no
'tention to what he's sayin'!*

"There ain't much paw and beller in a cowboy." "He ain't near so loquacious, nor frolicsome roun' strangers." "Among his own kind, he kin chin-jaw faster'n you kin spit and holler Howdy." "He don't do no fishin' round, for decirated words tuh make his meanin' clear." "He jaws less—larns more." "He sez a whole lot in a few words, but then it's been said the bigger the mouth the better it looks when it's shut."

Cowboy's don't sing, "They just open their mouths and WORDS fall out." **-Nathan "Jack" Howard Thorpe**

WASH DOWN THE TRAIL DUST

Music
Will McCain Clauson

Words
Howard "Chip" Culver
& Will McCain Clauson

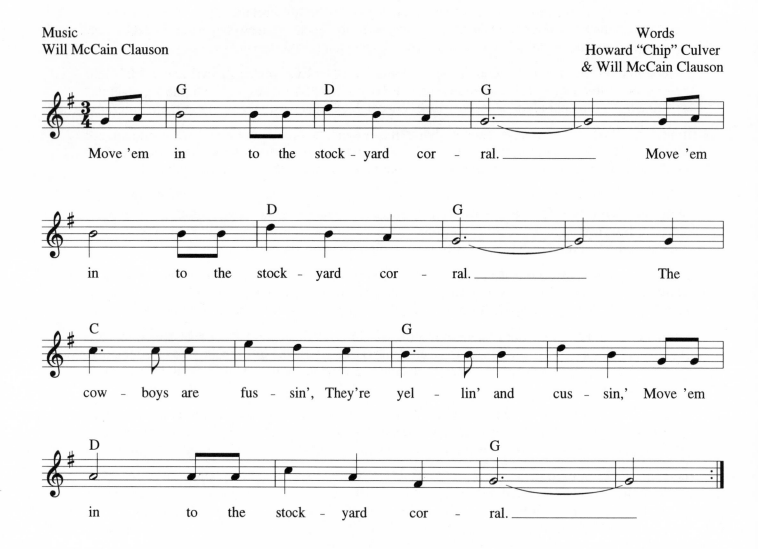

Move 'em in to the stock - yard cor - ral. _____ Move 'em

in to the stock - yard cor - ral. _____ The

cow - boys are fus - sin', They're yel - lin' and cus - sin,' Move 'em

in to the stock - yard cor - ral. _____

WASH DOWN THE TRAIL DUST

Move 'em in to the stockyard corral.
Move 'em in to the stockyard corral,
The cowboys are fussin'
They're yellin' and cussin'.
Move 'em in to the stockyard corral.

Prod 'em on up the chutes to the cars.
Prod 'em on up the chutes to the cars,
We're shippin' the cattle,
So, make the chutes rattle,
Prod 'em on up the chutes to the cars.
(Cont. next page)

Oh, the train won't be stayin' here long.
Oh, the train won't be stayin' here long,
It's leavin' the station,
To help feed the nation,
Oh, the train won't be stayin' here long.

When the train has pulled out with the herd.
When the train has pulled out with the herd,
The work will be over,
For the dusty ol' drover,
When the train has pulled out with the herd.

Then, we'll wash down the trail dust in town,
Then, we'll wash down the trail dust in town,
Where the girls will be waitin',
To help celebratin',
Where they wash down the trail dust in town.

We will all belly up to the bar.
We will all belly up to the bar,
We'll drink up the whiskey,
Where the girls are all frisky,
And they all belly up to the bar.

Note: Soloist may be accompanied by other singer(s) on second line of each verse.

COTTON, GINGHAM, LACE & CALICO

Words by Delores Wright

Cotton, gingham, lace and calico,
I'm goin' out with a brand new beau,
Momma says "Yes," Daddy says "No,"
But I'm goin' wear my new calico.

Cotton, gingham, lace and calico,
My hair's all shiny, tied up with a bow,
Patent leather shoes, and Momma's cameo,
I'm goin' out with a brand new beau.

Cotton, gingham, lace and calico,
Puttin' on my shawl, I'm ready to go,
We're goin' twirl till my petticoats show,
I'm steppin' out with my brand new beau.

Cotton, gingham, lace and calico,
Square dance, hoedown, heel and toe,
We won't come home till the roosters crow.
I'm goin' t'marry my brand new beau.

WAY OUT WEST IN KANSAS

Source: Waldo "Swede" Larson

Composed from Trad. Sources
Will McCain Clauson

The trains don't stop in my home town, The wood-peck-ers knocked the

de – pot down,_____ Out there the folks jes'

sit a-round, A – way out west in Kan - sas._____

Chorus

Way out in Kan - sas, _____ Way out in

Kan - sas,_____ Out there the folks jes'

sit a-round, A – way out west in Kan - sas._____

Reflectin' With An' Octogenarian Cowboy

*"Don't know whether I'd do it again, if I could...
but I would never want t' give up what I did."*

- Harold Tibbs

WAY OUT WEST IN KANSAS

The trains don't stop in my home town,
The woodpeckers knocked the depot down,
An' there the folks jes' sit around...
Away out west in Kansas.

Chorus:
Way out in Kansas, way out in Kansas;
Back there the folks jes' sit around,
Away out west in Kansas.

The folks ain't rich, they don't make scratch,
The sun's so hot that eggs'll hatch,
They'll pop right in your popcorn patch...
Away out west in Kansas.

The folks are poor, they live on air,
An' you can stand in the town square,
An' knock on every front door there...
Away out west in Kansas.

They chew tobacca, long an' thin,
That dribbles down upon their chin,
They lick it right back up again...
Away out west in Kansas.

I've gotta gal in Abilene,
Her eyes are wild, her look is mean*,
Crossed-eyedist gal ya ever seen...
Away out west in Kansas.

She cries because she's such wreck,
The tears run down the back of her neck,
She don't look straight to me, by heck...
Away out west in Kansas.

Out there the boys grow tall and thin,
Their ears turn out, their toes turn in,
They're in good shape, for the shape they're in...
Away out west in Kansas.

The gals are easy it's been said,
Don't give a dang if they are wed,
They'll kiss the boys and jump in bed...
Away out west in Kansas.

This song's the worst I ever writ,
The rhymes are bad, I must admit,
I'd better saddle up and git,
Away from good ol' Kansas.

Chorus:
Way out in Kansas, way out in Kansas,
I'd better saddle up and git,
Away from good ol' Kansas.

*This line contributed by Burt Jackson.

I admire the pioneer's uncanny ability to laugh at their own hardships and even joke about themselves and their conditions in songs as ludicrous as the one above.

WAY OUT ON THE CATTLE RANGE

Lyrics by J.B. Adams and Authors Unknown

Melody by Will McCain Clauson

WAY OUT ON THE CATTLE RANGE

The bawl of a steer to a cowboy's ear
is music of sweetest strain,
And the yelpin' notes of the wild coyotes
to him are a glad refrain;
The rapid beat of his bronco's feet
on the sod as he speeds along,
Keeps 'livenin' time to the ringin' rhyme
of his rollickin' cowboy song.
(Cont. next page)

(cont.)
Chorus:
Hal-e-o-hi-ay! to the range away,
On the deck of a bronc of steel,
With a careless flirt of a rawhide
quirt and the dig of a roweled heel.

His eyes are bright, and his heart is light
as the smoke of his cigarette,
There's never a care for his soul to bear,
no trouble to make 'im fret;
For a kingly crown in the noisy town
his saddle he would not change,
No life so free as the life we see
'way out on the cattle range.

Chorus:
Oh, the winds may howl and the thunder growl,
Or the breezes may softly moan,
The rider's life is the life for me,
The saddle a kingly throne.

At the long day's close, he his bronco throws
with the bunch in the hoss corral,
And a light he spies in the bright blue
eyes of his welcomin' rancher gal.
A light that tells of the love that dwells
in the soul of his little dear,
And a kiss he slips, to her waitin' lips,
when no one is watchin' near.

Chorus:
Hal-e-o-hi-ay! the work is play
When love's in the cowboy's eyes,
When his heart is light as the clouds of white,
That swim in the summer skies.

His glad thoughts stray to the comin' day
when away to the town they'll ride.
And the nuptial band by the parson's hand
will be placed on his bonnie bride.
And they'll gallop back to the old home shack,
to a life that is new and strange,
The cowboy bold, and the girl of gold,
the queen of the cattle range.

Chorus:
A cowboy song speeds the hours along
As he thinks of his little gal,
With the golden hair, who'll be waiting there
At the gate of the home corral.

134

WAY UP IN IDAHO

Words Traditional (Circa 1865)

Music by Will McCain Clauson

I know there is a land where cry - stal wa - ters flow, O'er beds of quartz and pu - rest gold, Way up in I - da - ho. Way up in I - da - ho, way up in I - da - ho, O'er beds of quartz and pu - rest gold, Way up in I - da - ho.

> *GOD PUT US ON EARTH*
> *TO GIT SOMETHIN' DONE.*
>
> *I'M SO FUR BEHIND RIGHT NOW,*
> *THERE AIN'T NO CHANCE OF ME DYIN'....*
> **-UNKNOWN**

WILDWOOD FLOWER

Joseph Philbrick Webster
(1819 - 1875)

Reverend Webster
Additional Words by
Will McCain Clauson

She would twine and would min – gle her rav – en black hair, With the

ros – es so red and the lil – ies so fair, And the myr – tle so green of an

em – er – ald hue, and the sweet em – a – ni – ta and is – lip so blue.

WILDWOOD FLOWER

She would twine and would mingle her raven black hair,
With the roses so red and the lilies so fair,
And the myrtle so green of an emerald hue,
And the sweet emanita and islip so blue.

*She would lie in my arms, changing midnight to dawn,
All her fears cast aside with her gown made of lawn.
She would pleasure and please me, my pale wildwood flower,
'Til we rose with the sun as it climbed to its tower.

Oh, she taught me to love her, my pale wildwood flower,
A rare blossom to treasure through life's every hour.
Now my flower has gone; gone and left me alone,
All the wildwood to weep, every wild bird to moan.

*Oh, how warm was her kiss in the cool wildwood bower,
But how cruel were the thorns of my pale wildwood flower.
Oh, how hollow the wildwood, how shallow the stream;
Oh, how quickly we wake at the end of a dream.
(Cont. next page)

136

(cont.)

Now I'll laugh and I'll sing, live my life without care,
All my troubles will vanish like motes in the air.
Oh, I'll live yet to see her regret this dark hour;
May she never forget me, my pale wildwood flower.

She would twine and would mingle her raven black hair,
With the roses so red and the lilies so fair,
And the myrtle so green of an emerald hue,
And the sweet emanita and islip so blue.

Every Southern mountain "picker" does a rendition of this song. You might be surprised to know, as I was, that it began life in 1860 as a parlor song. It was written by Joseph Philbrick Webster , who also wrote the music for the Civil War classic, "Lorena."

Authors have been writing words to this song ever since Rev. Webster (no relation to Philbrick) first penned the words. The original was meant to be sung as a girl's lament. I have only changed it so it would be possible for a male singer to use them as well.

* Authored by Clauson.

137

Cowboy Dances

The cowboy barn dances were infrequent, but when they were held, it was a foot stompin', thigh slappin', "gala affair." The Cowboy dance is the true folk dance of the last American frontier.

To the cattle range, and to the mining camps of the West, adventurers and fortune hunters came from every State of the Union, and brought with them the dances from their part of the country. The West became a free and open melting pot of American Folkways.

Folk dance scholars believe the three main sources of Western Dance came from the New England Quadrille, the Kentucky Running Set and the Mexican way of stepping, but their dances were not usually "called." Some of the steps of the cowboy dance are most certainly related to the European folk dances.

The most common instruments to accompany the cowboy dance were, first and foremost, the "fiddle" (violin), the bull fiddle (stand-up bass), a push button accordion, and/or a concertina. The banjo was used to a greater extent for dancing as it produced more volume than guitar. A honky-tonk "pie-anner" was found in most every Western saloon and also provided accompaniment for the dance.

What the musicians lacked in "concert" technique, they more than made up for in dexterity, endurance and in their "foot tappin'" rhythms and unique style of producing an incomparable sound.

The old time fiddler held his instrument at any angle that suited his individual fancy. Sometimes they wouldn't even bother to put the violin under their chin. Their bowing technique differs completely from that of the classical violinist. Even a certain amount of dissonance and slight "out-of-tuneness" is permissible.

"Fiddlers" mastered a proud craft all of their own, frowning on the "note readers." They learned to play the fiddle by ear from other old time fiddlers.

Some of the most popular dance tunes of the period were: "Rompin' Molly," "Buffalo Gals," "Soldier's Joy," "The Gal I Left Behind Me," "Cowboys and Indians," "Hens and Chickens," "Pigtown Hoe Down," "The So-So Polka" and, of course, "The Arkansas Traveler."

I have included some of these titles in the music section of this book. They are reproductions of authentic Frontier dance music.

"THANK YA," sounds good, but ya' cain't put WORDS in yer pocket.

-W M C

ARKANSAS TRAVELER

COWBOY AND INDIANS

DURANG

HENS 'N' CHICKENS

HULL'S VICTORY

GOLDEN SLIPPERS

I WONDER

FOUR WHITE HORSES

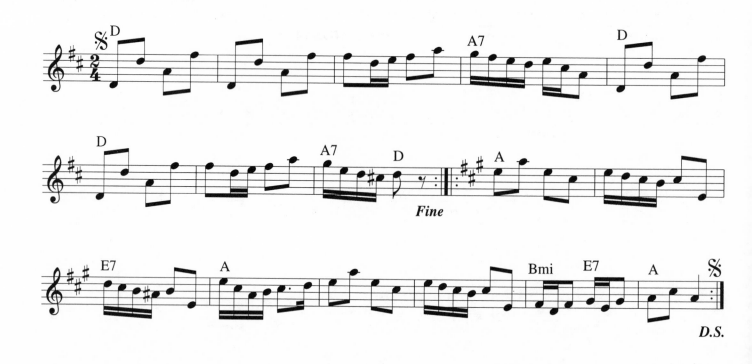

Fine

D.S.

WAGGONER

DEVIL'S DREAM

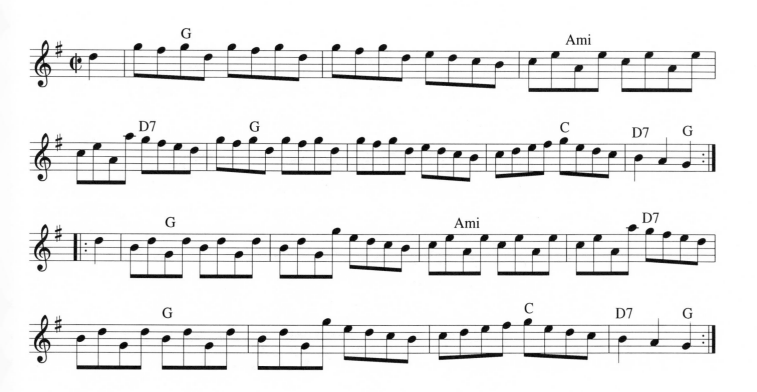

JOHNNY'S DOWN THE RIVER

ROMPIN' MOLLY

LAMP LIGHTER

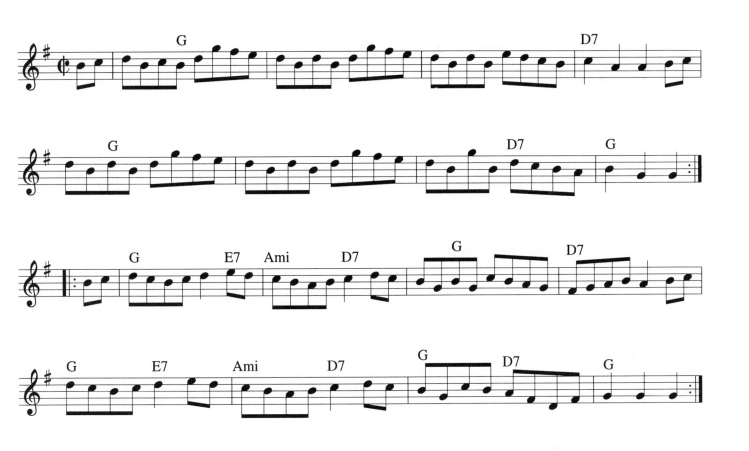

TURKEY IN THE STRAW

RYE WALTZ

SO - SO POLKA

OCEAN WAVES

WHITE COCKADE

SOLDIER'S JOY

PIGTOWN HOE-DOWN

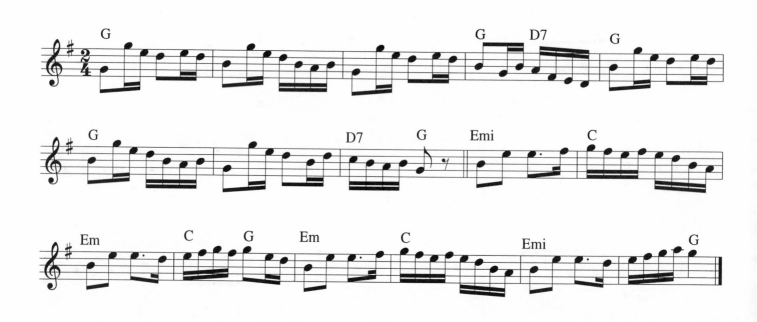

HO! WESTWARD, HO!
Soon the world shall know,
All is grand in the WESTERN land.
HO! WESTWARD, HO!

Western Expansion

"A hungry dog catches the rabbit," is an old pioneer saying. America, in those days, was made up of hungry people. Hungry for LAND, WEALTH, and FREEDOM, hungry to "git goin' an' doin'." They hungered for a PLACE for themselves where they could live in peace and contentment.

The pioneers, it seems, never allowed themselves to be completely satisfied at the place they found themselves. They might have built homes, started families and "tarried awhile," but in time, the urge to go on predominated. They "packed up" and "moved out" to see "what was on the other side of the hill."

Eastern "stay at homes" invented words and phrases to describe them and their ways. They had "wanderlust," "itchy feet," they were "rolling stones that gathered no moss" and they believed the "fields would be much greener" on the other side of the mountain.

Whatever that inherent motivation, without it, we can be sure the pioneers would not have continued westward as they did. They searched for better land, wealth in the California gold fields, and space to exercise religious freedom, all goals our human minds can understand. Reference was often made to a "promised land" as they pushed on to continue the search even though they knew in their hearts that nothing would satisfy completely the cravings of the soul.

They *"Sojourned in the Land of Promise,*
as in a strange country,"
"He (Abraham) looked for a city, which hath foundations,
whose builder and maker is God." **Hebrews 11:9-10**

"If ya' follow a new track there ain't no way of knowin'
If the man that made it knew where he was goin'!"
-Anon.

The prairie schooners that crossed the Great Plains, mountains and deserts brought a new breed of free spirited men and women to the far west. They were God fearing, independent, and self-determined to make a new life for themselves in a land of promises.

Before 1840, there was no West as we know it. The boundaries of the western frontier nation were continuously being pushed further toward the Pacific, even over seemingly impassable mountain ranges including the Alleghenies and Rockies. The first non-Indian explorers and trappers of the west included men such as Jim Beckwith, Benjamin Bonneville, Jim Bridger, Kit Carson, John Colter, John Fremont, Zebulon Smith, Jebediah Smith, and the Sublette Brothers. Many of the "mountain men" wandered the vast western wilderness in search of beaver pelts.

"The American claim is by rights of our Manifest Destiny to over-spread and
possess the whole of the Continent, the land which Providence has given us.
It is a right such as that of the tree to the space of air and earth suitable for the
full expansion of its principal destiny of growth."
- O'Sullivan

In 1845, journalist John Louis O'Sullivan penned the concept of "Manifest Destiny," whereby the citizens of the United States had a moral obligation and duty to vigorously pursue continental expansion. O'Sullivan's concept seemed to leap from the printed page into the American public's imagination and soul. The doctrine of "Manifest Destiny" more than implied that the national fulfillment for this quest for land was both a Divine right and with Divine approval.

(Cont. next page)

Between 1845 and 1848, the desire for expansion became almost obsessive. The discovery of gold in California in 1848 started another rush westward. Gold and silver fever spread from the "boomtowns" of the West cross country to the port cities of the East coast and to Europe. Other discoveries in the Colorado Rockies and Nevada mountains in the 1860-1870's further fueled the migrations.

Mining camps close to the "strikes" sprang up. The life of a miner was filled with shortages of the basic necessities such as food, clothing and shelter, but these were gladly suffered in the desire for the sudden wealth to be gained. Although the prospectors soon drifted on, they were replaced by those who had come to do business with them. Permanent settlements evolved as the little mining camps grew into boomtowns and then into cities.

In the beginning, the roads West were often no more than the temporary trails of the wolf and the buffalo, or the uncharted meandering of a shallow river bed, or canyon walls.

With whole families chafing to follow the sun came a greater need and demand for permanent and efficient forms of communication, and a great need for transportation between the States of the Republic and the Western Territories.

The U.S. annexed Texas, we almost had a war with Great Britain over Oregon, but, the peaceful agreement that followed brought new territorial additions. There was a war against Mexico, in which California and the great southwest became a part of our nation. The western expansion is, in essence, the history of our great nation.

The men and women who tamed and won the Old West, the Frontiersmen, the settlers, the adventurers, were visionaries who could look at a mountain range and see a water shed, look at a forest and see lumber for homes and stores; look at the plains and prairies covered by an endless sea of buffalo grass and see farms, towns and cities. They were brave, bold, ambitious, reckless and even violent at times, but fiercely determined to build a new life, a new world, and to live and thrive there in complete and glorious freedom.

By 1890, the pioneers, the forty-niners, the cattle rustlers, and the gun slingers had almost gone the way of the buffalo. The West of yesteryear is gone now and it is theirs forever. They have left their indelible mark on the roadway West. The tracks they have made upon the trail of history can never be blown away by the winds, or washed away by the rains. Their accomplishments so great and their deeds so durable, that they will for all eternity stand as a beacon light to the next generation of pioneers.

Women of the West

By pack horse, on foot, and in covered wagons, Women of America accompanied their families to the western wilds, playing a major role in the settling of the west. These mothers of the frontier, in their huge sun bonnets and faded gowns, fought alongside their husbands and brothers during Indian raids.

Thousands of women homesteaded their own land, and "women's work" meant any job that needed to be done. Women were not only strong bearers and nurturers of our traditions and family, pressing for the establishment of schools, churches and law and order, but they were also free spirited individuals who challenged convention by vying for, and filling competently, jobs that had historically been reserved for and performed by men. The western states and territories were the first to allow women to vote, and in the 1880's, to be elected to political office.

Women like the Nellie Cashman, whose luck in prospecting and business were only surpassed by her generosity to hospitals, church missions and "hard luck" prospectors. There were also are gamblers such as Eleanor Dumont and Pauline Cushman.

Women were only less than 10% of California's population in 1850. "With the later influx of women came also the graces of life, better social order and conditions, and increased regard for the amenities of existence," said an old miner who was there.

* Dr. Beardsley writes, "The life of women in the West was very hard, and only the strong survived. In the barren loneliness, some lost their minds. Others died young, yet, there was always great courage and beauty in these women. They were not a group of complaining martyrs, but builders of the West."

The women of the early West had to endure dawn to dark labor in home and field, be mate and home maker to their husbands, and bear his children, and raise a family under primitive conditions. They didn't have time, nor the luxury, of complaining even though some endured a decade or more of child bearing.

**They were the mistresses of all trades, making homes out of shacks. They gardened and worked the fields with their husbands. They spun the wool, wove the cloth and dyed it, and made the garments for the whole family. They cooked, nursed and taught, wrote letters and kept records, established schools and churches and participated in all of the activities that these involved.

> *FIFTY miles to WATER,*
> *A HUNDRED miles to WOOD,*
> *To Hell with this fool country,*
> *I'm goin' home fer GOOD.*
> **- Anon, 1865**

There was a shortage of wood and coal for cooking and heating, and often water was also scarce. Most of them were fine cooks, preparing food for their families on their wood burning stoves.

Despite hardships, the American West of the mid to late 19th century was a place of unparalleled opportunity. Missionaries Narcissa Whitman and Eliza Spalding were the first white women to cross over the Rocky Mountains. Doctors Sarah Hall, Mary Sawtelle and Bethenia Owens, successfully overcame the prejudice of both genders to practice medicine. Clara Shortridge Foltz and Laura Gordon, labored within the courts and halls of justice to win acceptance among the legal profession as attorneys. The author, Mary Foote was critically acclaimed as "the authentic voice of the West."

There were also those women, who like their male counterparts, sought fame and fortune in less reputable "professions" as ladies of the stage, actresses, and performers, such as wild and rowdy Lotta Crabtree and, the admired and beloved, Helena Modjeska. There were, of course, the "working girls," the soiled doves, the "fallen angels" and the madams. Many of them sweet and gentle souls who had merely gone astray.

Their names were as colorful as the time: Pearle de Vere, Josephine "Chicago Jo" Hensley, Julia Bulette, Contrary Mary, and Molly B'Damn. They were the ladies who "worked outside the law," rustlers and outlaws like Belle Starr and Big Nosed Kate, like Cattle Annie and Little Britches of the Doolan Gang and Pearl Heart, who "pulled off" the last stage coach hold up in the annals of the West.

One of the more colorful women of the West was Calamity Jane. She was a dashing, adventurous and rugged woman. She handled horses like a man, drove a stage coach from Miles City to Ekalaka, Montana, hitching the horses to the stage coach, putting the heavy harnesses on the horses by herself. She was given the nickname Calamity because she seemed accident prone.

"Arizona Mary" was also a bullwhacker who drove freight wagons pulled by oxen and mules the way a man did, by filling their ears with curses, and cracking a whip over their heads. "Old Charley" Parkhurst was a famous Wells Fargo driver. When "he" died in 1879, they discovered a well kept secret..."he" was a woman.

(Cont. next page)

There was a great scarcity of women in the cow country. They were held in high esteem and very rarely seen by the cowboy. This made him naturally shy. The only women he saw were the wives and daughters of the owner of the ranch he was working.

Most of the cow hands were unmarried and not ready to settle down anyway because of their young age and free roaming spirit. After the long trail drive, the female starved cowboy had no trouble in locating a bath, shave, and a "lady friend," as they were some times called.

Social gatherings and dances were infrequent, but when they happened they were a rompin', stompin' affair that might last, well chaperoned, until dawn. They provided the rare opportunity, as innocent as it may seem, for a cowboy to hold a lady in his arms while dancing.

* Source (this paragraph, preceding page) - **Arlene Giles**
** Source (next two paragraphs, preceding page) - **Arlene Giles**

Cowboy's Code of Ethics
Tips for the Puncher

Meet life head on—go after it. It's gotta be roped in a hurry so it don't git away.

Don't grumble, even if yer plumb sick an' tired. Remember—there ain't no room for a quitter's bed roll in the chuckwagon.

If yer guts turn to fiddle strings on the trail, it ain't no good fer you or the outfit. Courage is essential to survival on the range.

Don't ask a man his name if he don't give ya' one. Don't interfere with somethin' that ain't botherin' ya' none.

Yer expected to work long an' hard on the spring drive. No one ever drowned in his own sweat. Sleep in the winter. If ya' hire on, work for the man, an' ride for his brand. Treat his critters like ya' would yer own.

Ask no more an' give no less than yer best. Be loyal an' fair.

If ya' remove yer hat, do it in church. A tip of the brim is enough for the ladies.

Never miss a good chance to shut up. Talk low, talk slow, an' don't say too much. Talk less, learn more.

Don't wake a sleepin' cowpuncher, nor a critter, by touch. Use your voice to let 'em know you are gittin' near.

Never treat the new hand like a pardner, till ya' knows 'im. Never treat yer pardner like a new hand, or ya' might loose 'im.*

Take care of the horse you rode in on.

Drive the cattle slow, it's the only way they'll git there fast.

Be prepared for the unexpected an' unpredictable weather conditions. You might have to ride through heat or cold, blizzards or drought, an' against the drivin' wind an' sand. So be easy on the water, ya' never know if yer next waterin' hole has dried up. Rivers will have to be forded, with steers often flounderin' in quicksand. Be prepared for the other whims of nature, such as prairie fires caused by lightnin', blizzards an' snow storms.

If yer singin' on night guard, avoid the livelier tunes, stick to hymns an' ballads. The longhorns seem to find 'em more soothin'.

* Source: Amos Limognes

The following vividly describes an incident when a barroom suddenly became a courtroom.

NECKTIE JUSTICE

-Author Unknown

- Edited by Will McCain Clauson

A dusty cowpoke came one day,
To the store at Lone Star Station,
Lookin' for a few days work,
An' a little conversation.
He carried his bedroll, an' a sack,
An' added to his kitty,
Until he thought he had enough,
To leave for Carson City.

But one mistake the cowpoke made,
He paused at the barroom door,
Went inside, an' tossed his sack,
An' bedroll on the floor.
It landed with a clatter,
An' a odd metallic sound,
An' every man along the bar,
Turned curiously around.

"Leavin' us?" the barkeep asked.
"Yup, time to hit the road."
"That sack sounds heavy," someone said,
Fer such a small sized load.
"What's IN it?" an' they turned it OUT,
An' there upon the floor,
Were several cans of milk and jam,
He'd "borrowed" from the store.

"The dirty thief!" an' "Grab 'im boys!!"
The shoutin' noise, it grew,
The cowpoke eyed 'em nervously,
An' sipped his mountain dew,
"Let's string''im up!" "Whose gotta rope?"
"HOLD ON!!" the barkeep yelled.
The cowpoke has the RIGHT TO TRIAL,
I aim to see one held.

So, they choose up JUDGE and JURY,
In less than half a wink,
And then the cowpoke and the court,
Sat down fer another drink.
The AGENT was to prosecute,
The BARKEEP to defend,
The JUDGE gave his instructions,
Not hard to comprehend.

If "guilty," he'll be doomed to hang.
If innocent he's found,
He'll be assessed the costs of court,
He'll buy us DRINKS all 'round.
Though they were tempted to acquit,
They overcame the pang.
They pondered, found 'im guilty,
And SENTENCED 'im to HANG.

They tossed a rope across a beam,
An' dangled it in air,
They put a noose around his neck,
An' someone brought a chair.
As all hands grasped the tightened rope,
The barkeep's voice was heard,
"HOLD ON!!," this Pilgrim has a right,
To say his last an' final word.

The cowpoke spoke up grimly,
"To a better world—HERE GOES!!"
He leaped in space an' thrashed about,
While reachin' fur his toes.
Startled by this sudden turn,
The HANGMEN lost their hold.
The Cowpoke dropped down to the floor,
An' lay there...stretched out cold.

"Look what ya' done," the BARKEEP yelled.
He only stole some grub,
A man has to eat, even though he may be,
The lowest kind of scrub.
"We hung him once," the JUDGE decreed,
It's only common sense,
"You can HANG a man, but only ONCE,
At least for the same offense."

So they poured some Brandy down 'im,
An' ADDED to his PACK,
They shipped 'im off with a lusty cheer,
An' o'course he never came BACK!

153

In the frontier West, the SALOON was the first structure put up. It not only served as a theater for drinkin', gamblin', hurdy-gurdy girls, socializin' and fights, but a saloon would often serve as a hall of justice, barber shop, post office and even church.

THE BOYS 'R' BACK!

When we reached the Cowtown,
We drew our four months pay,
Times wuz so much better then,
They ain't like that today.

We'd all git drunk an' gamble,
An' swing the heifers 'round,
Shootin' an' a shoutin',
"THE BOYS 'R' BACK IN TOWN!"
-Anon, 1870

JUDGE ROY BEAN

He was born one day near Toyah,
Where he lairned t'be a Lawyah,
An' a Teacher, an' a Barber, an' a Mayor.
He was Cook, an' ol' Shoe Mender,
Sometimes Preacher, an' Bartender,
An' it cost two bits to have 'im cut yer hair!
-Anon.

Roy Bean represented "all the law West of the Pecos." He held court in his Saloon in Langtry, Texas.

Indians

In the beginning, the West belonged to the Indian and so it was for countless centuries until the white man came.

The first whites who moved West got along well with the "People of the Land," but in the late 1840's, as the trickle of emigrant wagon trains swelled into an endless sea of humanity, the Indians tolerance started to give way to anger, and they began taking up arms in defense of their ancestral lands.

With railroads to be constructed, homesteads to be claimed, towns to be built, and gold and silver to be mined, the United States government was charged with the safeguarding of any and/or all of its citizenry who desired to venture West.

By 1860, the U.S. government had executed over 350 treaties with the various tribes. Most of these documents acknowledged the sovereignty of the Indian Nations and recognized their title to their lands. Most of these agreements were designed for the express purpose of securing for the American government, title to the Indian lands in the Eastern section of the country in exchange for new "Indian lands in the West."

Promises of money and annual deliveries of food and supplies to the Indian signatories were generally included as part of the "bargain." More often than not, the treaties also guaranteed that the new lands out West would belong to the Indians forever.

All of these promises were broken. The tragic and devastating conflict that developed between the Western Indians and the expanding American nation was fore-ordained by the two peoples vast conceptual and cultural differences regarding the use and ownership of "The Land."

The Native Americans believed the land they roamed freely belonged to all. No individual Indian would dream of claiming personal ownership of a plot of ground. "The Land" was a source of identity and "the people" were only one small part of the larger natural order that lived on it.

"The Land," and all of its inhabitants, both man and beast, were to be respected and revered. "The Great Spirit" expected the "earth's bounty" to be judicially harvested and conscientiously conserved by mankind. Resources must be allowed to restore and replenish in order that there would always be plenty.

The "white man" saw "The Land" in terms of material object; a personal possession, to be bought and sold, owned and exploited, used and abused as the "owner" saw fit. This philosophical and ecological difference of opinions between the "red" and "white" men led to nearly a half a century of bloody and savage warfare.

The human travesty known as the "Indian Wars" began in 1854, with the butchering of a settler's cow by a starving Native, and ended in 1890 with the butchering of 150 Indian men, women and children by U.S. Military forces in the dead of winter at a place called Wounded Knee.

From the pages of history came the voices of the great Chiefs who sought peace and understanding between these two diverse cultures.

> *"The white man who possess this whole vast country from sea to sea, who roams over it at pleasure, and lives where he likes cannot know the cramp we feel in this little spot, with undying remembrance of the fact...that every foot of what you call America, not very long ago belonged to the red man."*
> **Chief Washakie of the Shoshone**

> *"It is cold, and we have no blankets. The little children are freezing to death...I am tired, my heart is sick and sad."*
> **Chief Joseph of the Nez Perce**

> *"God almighty has made us all and he is here to bless what I have to say to you today. I am a representative of the original American race, the first people of this continent. We have given you all of our lands and if we had any more land to give, we would give it. We have nothing more."*
> **Chief Red Cloud of the Sioux**

As this new race flooded the West, the Indians were herded onto reservations, and when this land was found to be rich in timber, minerals and farm ground, they were pushed onto the poorest land. Those who chose to fight were killed or exiled to the Oklahoma Indian territory.

The buffalo were killed, the rivers dammed and the salmon stopped running. The virgin soil was tilled, roads built and cities created.

Protestant and Catholic missionaries came to "teach the Indian," not only reading, writing, and farming, but to convert them to the white man's religion. In 1847, the Bureau of Catholic Indian Missions was formed, and was instrumental in getting more humane treatment of the Indians by Congress. By the late 1880's, however, the Indian's true way of life was doomed.

(Cont. next page)

As an ever increasing human tide flowed across the Northern plains and breached the mountain passes leading to the "Promised Lands" of Oregon and California, a young nation set out to tame the far west. At first explorers, followed by mountain men, homesteaders, gold seekers, cavalry, cowboys, railroaders, gamblers, con men, merchants, and drifting adventurers prevailed against nature and the native inhabitants of the new land, and imposed the codes of white civilization.

The INDIAN WAY:
If it CANNOT be changed, it MUST be accepted.
-Source Arlene Giles

Buffalo

Before the Indians had horses, they would run the buffalo over cliffs, which we came to call buffalo jumps. The buffalo was a vast store house of goods for the Indian. They wasted nothing, and a use was found for every part. When the buffalo was hunted to extinction by the white man, the Indian lost not only their way of life but also their means of sustaining it.

THE MONARCH OF THE PLAINS
Gone are the days of the buffalo.
It fills my heart with pain,
To know them days are past and gone,
To never come again.
-Anon.

Gunfighters

One afternoon he rode along,
Across the Texas plain,
The hungry buzzards flew above,
As he calmly held his rein.
When suddenly he heard a shout,
"Surrender, or you're done!"
"Then fight, for I'll not yield!" Matt cried,
THAT GALLANT IRISH SON.
- From the poem "Matt Guiness," by Basil Swift

Lawlessness (the outlaws and the rough and tumble gun slingin' cowpokes) were a part of the Old West, a part that would have prevailed without the strong, fast hands of such ledgendary lawmen as Wild Bill Hickok, Pat Garret and Wyatt Earp. The local Sheriff often called for their assistance whenever The Hole in The Wall Gang, the Clantons, the James Brothers or the Youngers came to town.

The "draw-shoot" era came into being after the Civil War. Outlaws, killers, and train robbers were called the "bad men" of the Old West. They were known and feared, quick on the draw, and deadly shots. Many of these men showed cowardly traits, using trickery and surprise, and were not thought of as brave.

They held up trains, rustled cattle and took any side for pay in some of the bloody cattle wars. They were either shot down, with their boots on, or swung eventually from a rope over a limb. They hid out in mountain regions as members of gangs. Many of the best lawmen of the period began their careers as outlaws. And even later, it seems they sometimes had one foot on each side of the law.

Many of the top gunfighters were related, Jesse James to the Youngers, the Youngers to the Daltons, and Cole Younger, the Uncle of John Ringo. John Wesley Hardin had relatives all over Texas. Rail head towns of the cattle drives also brought the gunslinger out. This period of history, when the "waistband of death" ruled the West, lasted less than twenty years.

The quick draw shoot out, where two gun fighters "faced off," has been overly exaggerated. A frontier gunman, intent on killing his rival or victim usually did so covertly by ambush. Shooting a man in the back was common, and most of the gunslingers "died with their boots on." Something more common was two cowboys "facing off" in a chin-jawin' contest. They would each "air their lungs" until one or the other, or both, finally ran out of words or wind.

CLAY ALLISON: Born 1840 - Accidentally crushed to death, 1877.

WILLIAM BARCLAY (BAT MASTERSON): Born 1856 - Cashed in his chips in 1921 of natural causes.

"BILLY THE KID" WILLIAM BONNEY: Born 1859 - died 1881, killed by Pat Garrett. In Hico, Texas, they celebrate "Billy the Kid Days," claiming he died there of a heart attack, after he was well past the age of 90!

CURLEY BILL BROCIOUS: Birth unknown - Died 1882, killed by Wyatt Earp.

MARTHA JANE CANARY (CALAMITY JANE): Born about 1848, Princeton, Missouri - Died 1903, buried next to Wild Bill Hickok in Deadwood, S.D.

BUTCH CASSIDY: Born 1867, died in 1936, natural causes. Some believe he died in a gun fight with troops in South America.

N. H. CLANTON: Born about 1830 - Killed at O.K. Corral shootout in 1882.

JIM COURTRIGHT: Born 1848 - Killed by Luke Short in 1887.

WYATT EARP: Born in Monmouth, Illinois about 1848 - Died with his boots OFF at the age of 81.

The NICHOLAS EARP family, with their five boys and three girls, traveled from Pella, Iowa, by covered wagon and settled on a ranch near Redlands, California, along the Santa Ana River. The boys were MORGAN, VIRGIL, JAMES, WARREN and WYATT. Colton can claim to be the "home of the Earps," as most of the family resided, or spent a great deal of time, around this area.

WYATT EARP was sixteen years of age when they arrived and before he was eighteen, was driving a six horse team for Phinneas Banning, owner of Banning Stage Line. Young WYATT drove from Banning to San Bernadino, through Colton into Los Angeles, and back each day, seven days a week.

After his short lived career as a stage driver, EARP became a famous lawman and moved on to more exciting things such as gambling, prospecting and land speculation. He was, for a time, a Wells Fargo detective and made a name for himself in Tombstone, Arizona, as a deputy under his brother, VIRGIL, who was the town's Police Chief.

Along with his brothers, and "DOC" HOLLIDAY, he immortalized himself in the 1881 shoot out at O.K. Corral. Brothers TOM and FRANK MC LAURY and BILLY CLANTON met their doom on that fateful day. IKE CLANTON escaped by diving into a doorway just ahead of a blast from "DOC" HOLLIDAY's shotgun. MORGAN, VIRGIL and "DOC" were wounded. In the same year, VIRGIL's left arm was shattered by a retaliatory shotgun blast, and in March, 1882, MORGAN was killed in an ambush.

Soon thereafter, EARP migrated North to Kootenai County, Idaho. He operated the White Elephant Saloon with his brothers. He was also active in locating and acquiring gold claims, filing on at least three claims in and near the Eagle City-Murray mining district. Claim jumping and "mis-filed" claims were rampant during this period and it seems that WYATT was not immune to "positioning himself favorably" in several instances. They took the Marshal-Saloon Keeper to court rather than having it settled by gun. Wyatt won only one court case, he lost money, and abandoned the White Elephant, losing the saloon for the amount of $8.00 due in taxes. After his North Idaho misfortunes, he left for Texas.

(Cont. next page)

He was married three times, the last being "dubiously so" to Josephine, a former Lady of the Evening, who traveled with the brothers over the years and was not widely accepted in the clan. In contrast to the average life span of gunman, WYATT EARP lived to the ripe old age of 81.

KING FISHER: Born 1854 - Killed along with Ben Thompson, 1884.

PAT GARRETT: Born in the deep South in 1850 - Killed 1908 by Wayne Brazil.

JOHN WESLEY HARDIN: Born 1853 - Son of a preacher - Shot in the back, 1895.

JAMES BUTLER HICKOK: Born 1837 - Killed 1876, in Deadwood, S.D.

DOC HOLIDAY: Born in Valdosta, Georgia about 1852 - Son of a Confederate Army Major - Died 1887 of natural causes.

JESSE JAMES: Born 1847 - Son of a Baptist minister, killed by a former member of his gang, Bob Ford, in 1882.

> *When he was but a lad,*
> *He rode with Quantrill,*
> *He robbed the Glendale train.*
> *He stole from the rich,*
> *An' gave to the poor,*
> *He'd never see a man suffer pain.*
>
> *The people held their breath,*
> *When they heard of Jesse's death,*
> *An' wondered how Jesse came to die.*
> *It was one of the gang,*
> *By the name of Bobby Ford,*
> *That shot poor Jesse James on the sly.*
> **- Billy Gashade, circa 1882**

According to the museum in Stanton, Missouri, the man killed was Charlie Bigelow, a member of the James Gang. It was supposedly all a hoax, perpetrated for the purpose of permitting James to assume another name and escape the consequences of his deeds. They claim that the Governor of Missouri at the time, T. T. Critenden, was in on the plot.

Jesse Woodson James, alias J. Frank Dalton, died in Granbury, Texas, August 16, 1951, at the age 103 years, eleven months and ten days. In 1948, when "Dalton" first came forward, some of the other members of the James Gang were still alive. They all supported the fact that "Dalton" was indeed James. During the course of interviews with Dalton from 1948 - 1951, no one could ever prove he was not Jesse James.

BILL LONGELY: Born in Austin County, Texas 1851 - His father was in Sam Houston's Army - Hung at 27 years of age, 1878.

ETTA PLACE: Died of natural causes in 1949.

JOHN RINGO: Born in Texas, 1844 - Died 1882, ambushed and killed.

LUKE SHORT: Born in Texas about 1854 - Died on his sick bed in 1893.

BELLE STARR: Born 1848 - murdered, February 3, 1889. She was shot in the back by an unknown assasin. Nathan Thorpe, who knew the "Bandit Queen" personally, reputedly obtained a poem "My Love Was A Rider," a version of which you will find in this book.

"THE SUNDANCE KID" HARRY LONGABAUGH: Born in Cook County, Wyoming. Buried in Casper, Wyoming and died of natural causes in 1958 at the age of 98, according to his son, Harry Junior, who saw and talked to him the last time in 1947.*

BEN THOMPSON: Born in 1843 in Lockhard, Texas - Killed at the age of forty-one.

* Harry Longabaugh, Jr., died in a hotel fire in Missoula, Montana, in 1972. He gave a lecture at the Weber County Library June 24, 1970, which was taped, and from which I have gathered the above information.

GLOSSARY

Assafidity bag: What people wore around their necks containing strange smelling herbs
Barkin' twelve: shotgun
Bean Master: cook
Box knocker: Banjo player
Clabberin' up to rain: clouding up for rain
Corpse maker: killer
Coulee: a branch or side prong of a draw, i.e. a small draw
Cow paste: butter
Demijohn: Little Brown Jug
Draw: a dry creek-bed running from the divide to the main creek, the draw carries water only when it rains, and serves as a catch basin for the slopes when it rains. It shelters the cattle from the summer heat and winter cold. The draws must be thoroughly combed in order to find all the cattle.
Duce: smoking tobacco
Finer 'n' frog hair, cut and quartered: something really good
Fraggle: to steal
Go squirlin': to go shooting
Grin-hole: the mouth
Hard to find as a rainbow in a flour bin: something hard to find
Havin' the peedoodles: being nervous
Lucifers: matches
Mean enough to bite himself: nasty
Mouth-almighty: Bragger
Mud kickers: boots
Muddin' the catch: packing wrapped fish in mud to bake in the ground
Onion head: bald headed man
Paddin' out yer belly: eating too much
Phoo-phoo: perfume
Pill roller: doctor
Plug of duce: chewing tobacco
Puttin' the iron to the hide: branding
Puttin' on the nose bag: eating
Sassengers: sausages
Skunk eggs: onions
Sky juice: water
Stompin' the churn: using the butter churn
Squitzys: squirrels
Swing the latch: close the door
To scally-hoot: leave in a hurry
Vittles: food
Whompin' the carpet: beating the carpet or quilts to remove dust
Wisdom bringer: school teacher

Pioneer tips:Use rain water to wash hair, and Skunk oil for head colds

**Portions of the glossary were provided by Chuck Wright